Praise for

Women and War

"*Women and War* offers a state-of-the-art look at how war affects women and women affect war—and peace. The collection surveys the burgeoning literature on gender and armed conflict, adding original research showing the yawning gap between international commitments (like UN Resolution 1325) and the brutal realities facing women amid war. It does so with a nuanced view of the differential impacts of war on women's bodies, social circumstances, and economic chances. Fully recognizing the agency of women and their contributions to peacemaking, peacekeeping, and postwar economic development, this book doesn't shy away from identifying flawed international approaches and persistent obstacles that block women's potential roles in peace and economic recovery. Kuehnast, Oudraat, and Hernes have given practitioners, scholars, and students an indispensable new resource."
—**Charles T. Call,** American University

"News headlines indicate that the victimization of women in war is often a deliberate policy of the belligerents and even a by-product of the well-intentioned stabilization efforts of outsiders. Yet this phenomenon remains understudied by the academic community and not well understood by policymakers who seek to limit the consequences of conflicts. This policy-oriented book aims to help fill the academic gap with informative chapters that move beyond the anecdotal to provide foundational data on the victimization of women. It traces the efforts—slow and halting at the operational levels—of the member states of the United Nations to put forward the rights of women. It offers a well-thought-out agenda for action premised on the proposition that being gender-neutral discriminates against women. This volume should be read not only by those concerned with the victimization of women in war and peace processes but also by those who do not yet fully appreciate the depth of the problem."
—**Don Daniel,** Georgetown University

"I have met too many survivors of sexual violence in the Congo, Darfur, Bosnia, Kosovo, Uganda, Colombia, and elsewhere. For too long we have tolerated that a conspiracy of silence surround mass rape of women in war. This colossal injustice is as old as war itself, but it is only now starting to be addressed. *Women and War* from USIP and PRIO should get more of

us who can live without fear and shame to wake up, be outraged, and act for change."
—**Jan Egeland,** director of the Norwegian Institute of International Affairs and former UN Undersecretary General for Humanitarian Affairs

"*Women and War* should be on the desk of every mediator, peacekeeper, and policymaker working in the international peace and conflict arena. The book uses empirical evidence to cut its way through stereotypes of women as victims of war, taking us on a vivid journey of women's actual experiences, ranging from the rape camps of Kosovo to the surprising effects of a gender-neutral peace in Angola. The authors shed light on the triumphs and failures of UN Security Council Resolution 1325, and provide a road map for the full participation of women at all stages of peacebuilding. The book is sure to make readers question deep-seated assumptions about the roles of women, and will change how we all think about war, peace, and justice."
—**Melanie Greenberg,** president, Cypress Fund for Peace and Security and Co-President, Women in International Security

"*Women and War* provides a long-neglected analysis of the role of women in conflict not only in their absence from the decision-making process, but also in the impact of conflict on women and the broader society. In the case of the latter, the book makes a compelling case that unlike past tendencies to regard women as passive, women often assume leadership roles within their families as well as their communities to the point of active combatants. For scholars, this book breaks ground with respect to the critical role of women and is an essential book for students as well."
—**Gale Mattox,** Georgetown University and U.S. Naval Academy

"*Women and War* illuminates the toll that war takes on women and the role that women's empowerment can play in reducing the horrors of war. This well-designed volume combines incisive analysis and rich factual detail with practical take-home lessons."
—**Jack Snyder,** Belfer Professor of International Relations, Columbia University

"*Women and War* makes a truly noteworthy contribution to our understanding of gender's sculpting impact on conflict. In clear and passionate prose, the authors spotlight the various impacts and yawning gaps in how Resolution 1325 is being interpreted and applied a decade after its adoption. Superb considerations of sexual violence and the economic chal-

lenges confronting women in postwar worlds set Resolution 1325 into essential context. Anyone aiming to grasp the commanding imprint of gender on war and peacebuilding will find *Women and War* essential reading."
—**Marc Sommers,** The Fletcher School, Tufts University

"Peace agreements typically fall apart when they fail to resolve the issues that caused the conflict in the first place—including ethnic tensions, inequality, and injustice. Women face these problems everyday so they should be the ones who bring these issues to the negotiating table and find practical solutions. I believe that this book, which explores important themes such as women's security, peacebuilding by women, and violence against women, is highly relevant as we mark the tenth anniversary of UN Security Council Resolution 1325 on Women, Peace, and Security."
— **Jonas Gahr Støre,** Norwegian foreign minister

Women and War

Women and War

Power and Protection in the 21ˢᵗ Century

Kathleen Kuehnast,
Chantal de Jonge Oudraat,
and
Helga Hernes
Editors

UNITED STATES INSTITUTE OF PEACE PRESS
WASHINGTON, D.C.

UNITED STATES INSTITUTE OF PEACE
2301 Constitution Avenue, NW
Washington, DC 20037
www.usip.org

First published 2011

To request permission to photocopy or reprint materials for course use, contact the Copyright Clearance Center at www.copyright.com. For print, electronic media, and all other subsidiary rights e-mail permissions@usip.org.

Printed in the United States of America

The paper used in this publication meets the minimum requirements of American National Standards for Information Science—Permanence of Paper for Printed Library Materials, ANSI Z39.48-1984.

Library of Congress Cataloging-in-Publication Data

Women and war : power and protection in the 21st century / Kathleen Kuehnast, Chantal de Jonge Oudraat, and Helga Hernes, editors.
    p.   cm.
Includes index.
ISBN 978-1-60127-064-1 (pbk.)
    1. Women and war.   2. Women and peace.   3. War crimes.
4. Women—Crimes against.   I. Kuehnast, Kathleen R.
II. de Jonge Oudraat, Chantal.   III. Hernes, Helga.
    JZ6405.W66W66   2011
    362.87082—dc22
                                        2010038337

Contents

Acknowledgments

This volume would not have seen the light of day without the help of many colleagues and friends of the U.S. Institute of Peace (USIP) and the Peace Research Institute of Oslo (PRIO). Since one of the goals of our book is to further trans-Atlantic collaboration, the editors want to thank several key individuals who played a pivotal role in their early support of this collaboration, namely Robert Dresen (Royal Embassy of the Netherlands), Torunn Lise Tryggestad (PRIO), Elizabeth Cole (USIP), and the Gender Working Group (USIP). The editors held a preliminary manuscript meeting in The Hague in December 2009 and would like to thank our host, Christa Meindersma of the Hague Institute for Strategic Studies. An authors' meeting in late March 2010 in Washington, D.C., at the U.S. Institute of Peace provided considerable input and guidance for the next round of revisions. For this, special thanks go to the reviewers and commentators, including Maria Correia of the World Bank, Carla Koppell of the Institute for Inclusive Security, Jolynn Shoemaker of Women in International Security (WIIS), and Marc Sommers, a former Jennings Randolph Senior Fellow at USIP. In addition, our colleagues at USIP, Pamela Aall, Virginia Bouvier, Raymond Gilpin, Vivienne O'Connor, Robert Perito, Colette Rausch, and Abiodun Williams provided invaluable input and support. With any manuscript, the often invisible but indispensible assistance must be acknowledged; in this case, we especially recognize Nina Sudhakar, Shira Lowinger, Janene Sawers, Ryan McClanahan, and Brooke Stedman. We would also like to thank the director of the USIP Press, Valerie Norville, and her staff, especially Michelle Slavin. A round of thank-yous to Wendy Muto, the editing manager. Finally, a special word of thanks goes to the leadership of PRIO and USIP, particularly Tara Sonenshine for her unwavering support, as well as to the leadership of PRIO, particularly Kristian Berg Harpviken. In conclusion, the editors would like to extend a special thanks to the authors, Sanam Anderlini, Tilman Brück, Inger Skjelsbæk, Donald Steinberg, Marc Vothknecht, and Elisabeth Wood, for their enthusiasm and willingness to embrace the rapid-paced production schedule, and the good nature with which they accepted comments and revisions through-out the process. We hope that this book will prompt thoughtful action and stimulate relevant research on the roles of women in maintaining, and where necessary, restoring international peace and security. The agenda is vast and the need urgent.

The editors,

Kathleen Kuehnast, Chantal de Jonge Oudraat, and Helga Hernes

1

Introduction

Kathleen Kuehnast, Chantal de Jonge Oudraat,
and Helga Hernes

For most of the twentieth century the study and practice of war and international relations were dominated by men and focused on the security of states. The end of the Cold War and the changing nature of violent conflict—in particular, the unique and formidable challenges posed by intrastate conflicts—have changed the way in which policymakers and experts think about war and its impacts. At the conceptual level we have witnessed a shift from a perspective that sees security solely through a military lens and thus emphasized the security of states to a perspective that takes into account nonmilitary aspects of security, drawing on the notion of human security to focus on the individual and relations between individuals and groups within societies. This changed perspective has also led to greater awareness of the role of gender in international relations. At the operational level, we have witnessed a call for a more active role for the United Nations and greater sensitivity to the specific challenges faced by women in conflict situations.

The Fourth World Conference on Women, held in Beijing in 1995, brought the impact of war on women's lives and the issue of women's agency in international and national security issues to the attention of world leaders.[1] Five years later, they adopted UN Security Council Resolution (UNSCR) 1325. By recognizing the importance of the role of

---

1. Until 1995 the global conferences on women had focused on economic development issues.

women in preventing and resolving violent conflict, the members of the Security Council handed civil society organizations and women peace activists from around the world a major victory and an authoritative instrument for further mobilization. At the heart of the resolution are two main ideas. First, women must have the power to participate equally in all efforts to maintain and promote peace and security. The resolution recognized that women were largely absent from decision-making processes related to conflict prevention and resolution and that their role must be increased. Only the full and equal participation of both men and women could provide a sustainable and lasting peace. Second, world leaders recognized that women are more exposed to physical violence than men, especially in intrastate conflicts, and that they bear inordinate burdens during conflict. Hence, special efforts need to be made to protect them from physical violence—sexual violence, in particular—and to help them overcome the burdens imposed by war.

Since the adoption of UNSCR 1325, many states, international organizations, non-governmental organizations (NGOs), and academic institutions have undertaken many activities, including the elaboration of action plans, policies, and guidelines to ensure that women have equal and fair representation at operational and decision-making levels and be extended specific measures to guarantee their protection from physical harm—sexual violence, in particular. In sum, Resolution 1325 has become a powerful tool for those advocating for gender equality (gender balancing) and greater sensitivity to gender issues (gender mainstreaming). That said, stereotypical thinking about men and women in the international peace and security realm is persistent, and much remains to be done at both the conceptual and operational levels.

In this introductory chapter we do three things. First, we briefly review the state of the field—that is, we examine current thinking about the role of gender in the international security realm. The literature on this issue, while growing, remains on the margins of the international security studies field and suffers from the lack of good empirical data. Second, we briefly examine the situation of women in the field—that is, the way international actors have dealt with the particular role of women during and after violent conflict. We look in particular at how gender sensitivity has affected the situation of women in refugee camps, peace operations, and post-conflict reforms of the security sector. Again, much progress has been made, but more remains to be done. Lastly, we provide a road map to this volume and offer guidance for the road ahead.

Women and War: The State of the Field

In linking women's experiences of conflict to the international peace and security agenda, UNSCR 1325 recognizes gender to be a key issue for conflict analysis. That said, there is a lot of confusion and lack of understanding about the role of gender in conflict. Indeed, much of the literature on conflict and security depicts women as passive victims.

Recent research on women and conflict challenges this view and presents a more comprehensive and nuanced understanding of the varied roles of women in conflict. Caroline Moser and Fiona Clark (2001), for example, have highlighted the different roles that women play in conflict. The essays in their edited volume show that women often do not remain passive spectators during a war, or simply innocent victims, as once thought. Rather, they take on new roles and responsibilities, often participating in violent struggles as active combatants, or taking on the role of provider for their families by obtaining resources and building networks of support. The essays in Krishna Kumar's collection (2001) emphasize that though war places a heavy burden on women and may exact disproportionate costs from them, conflict may also help redefine traditional roles and reconfigure existing gender relations within society.

Conflict analysis that takes gender into account has also come to distinguish between women's roles before, during, and after conflict by focusing on societal inequalities that exist in access to and control over resources and participation in decision making at different points within the conflict cycle. For example, Tsjeard Bouta and Georg Frerks (2002) have proposed a framework identifying seven different roles that women may play in internal conflicts. They may be victims of (sexual) violence, combatants, peace activists in the non-governmental sector, actors in formal peace politics, coping and surviving actors, household heads, and/or employed in the formal or informal economic sectors. Combinations of these roles may also occur.

Others have stressed that more active roles of women are dependent on national, socioeconomic, and cultural contexts and often will fail without broader social transformations (Afshar and Eade 2003). For example, attention paid to women only during the post-conflict period may come too late to transform patriarchal gender relations (Meintjes, Turshen, and Pillay 2002). Projects focused on women in war, then, should take into account both the underlying gendered power relations that affected women's roles before the conflict broke out and the dynamics of social change that occur over the conflict cycle (Afshar and Eade 2003). Tsjeard Bouta, Georg Frerks, and Ian Bannon (2004) have suggested that policies and projects that introduce gender equality and notions of inclusion must, in order to be effective, capitalize on gains made by women during wartime. Conflict presents an opportunity to encourage change and build more inclusive and gender-balanced social, economic, and political power relations in post-conflict societies. In addition, it has been argued that inclusive policies that engage women and youth and tackle underlying structural causes and power relations will result in more effective and long-term peaceful relations (Baksh-Sodeen 2005).

Efforts to end war and prevent its recurrence also need to provide the means for women to be active participants in building an inclusive, peaceful society. Indeed, those who assume power in the aftermath of war are the actors who create the social, political, and economic conditions within which such power is maintained (Mazurana, Raven-Roberts, and Parpart 2005). The marginalization of gender as a "soft" issue in conflict resolution and reconstruction can thus perpetuate or re-create societal inequalities that encourage conflict. In order to achieve sustainable peace, gender equality and gender discrimination issues should be regarded as essential components of post-conflict reconstruction projects (Greenberg and Zuckerman 2006). Elaine Zuckerman and Marcia Greenberg (2004) recommend a framework for post-conflict reconstruction work that addresses gender through a rights-based approach, identifying the kinds of rights that must be guaranteed to women in the post-conflict period. These include not only the right to participate in policymaking and resource allocation but also the right to benefit equally from those resources and services.

In spite of these advances in our understanding of the role of gender in conflict and post-conflict situations, gendered analyses of international relations and conflict situations remain marginal and outside the mainstream. This state of affairs has practical consequences, as Donald Steinberg explains in the concluding chapter of this volume. He recalls how the 1994 "gender-neutral" peace accords to end the civil war in Angola lacked provisions requiring the participation of women in the implementation bodies, and as a result "issues such as sexual violence, human trafficking, abuses by government and rebel security forces, reproductive health care, and girls' education were given short shrift, if addressed at all." Similarly, the amnesty provisions showed Angolan women that the peace process was intended for the ex-combatants and not for the women subject to sexual abuse during the war. He reminds us that gender-neutral peace accords not only neglect the voices of women, they also fail to recognize that such neglect ultimately undermines the peace. Similarly, many observers worry that talks about reconciliation with the Taliban in Afghanistan will ignore gender issues and shortchange women's rights (Hassan 2010).

Disregard of women's basic human rights, such as protection from sexual abuse and access to education and work, will result in women's continued relegation to subordinate positions in the home and private sphere and the perpetuation of their being marginalized in the public sphere. Many feminist theorists argue that unless the unequal power relations between men and women are dealt with, insecurities and violent conflict will persist. A "sustainable peace requires a more permanent transformation of social norms around violence, gender and power" (Sarosi 2007, 1). As Susan Willett contends, "Gender hierarchies are socially constructed, and maintained, through power structures that work against women's participation in foreign and national security policymaking" (Willett 2010, 145; see also Tickner 2001). Ignoring these structures will only preserve relationships of oppression and subordination. Indeed, many women engaged in peace talks will frequently remind their Western interlocutors that ending the war often does not stop the violence.

The lack of attention in academic circles to the notion of gender and the role of women in international security, as well as the refusal to seriously examine gender as an analytical concept and a unit of analysis, is in the first instance a resistance to envisaging alternatives to traditional notions of security. For many academics and policymakers, security continues to be defined primarily in military terms and connected to the notion of the state. A worldview that remains prisoner of a Hobbesian and Westphalian conception of power has little to say about gender or the particular role of women in international peace and security. As long as these dominant frameworks stay in place, scant progress can be made in understanding what goes on in today's predominant form of violent conflict— namely, internal conflict. We believe that an effective conflict prevention and conflict management strategy must bring into focus the gendered reality of international relations and explore the complex web of power inequalities operating within and across the sexes.

The Lack of Data

The marginalization of gendered analyses in international peace and security studies has meant that the research agenda on these issues remains underdeveloped. International and national nongovernmental organizations have been more active in this realm and have provided a wealth of data on the experiences of women in war—but much of this material is anecdotal and lacks a systematic and analytical focus. The absence of systematically collected data is repeatedly lamented in the chapters in this volume.

The problem of accurate and reliable data is particularly acute when considering conflict casualty data—a key indicator for the severity of a conflict. There are many institutions that track deaths resulting from violent conflict. Each of these institutions has its own set of drivers and rationales for collecting data. Hence, they collect different types of data and use different methodologies. For example, the military focuses on military casualties and collects wartime casualty data—that is, they monitor the direct effects of combat and combat-related exposures.[2] NGOs and relief agencies, on the other hand, often focus on civilians and collect data about broader causes of death.[3] Finally, academics might collect death-related data to uncover trends with regard to violent conflicts over time. They will generally adhere to strict definitions of violent conflict, using criteria of fatality thresholds and time frames, but those definitions themselves can vary widely, ranging from 1,000 deaths per year to 100 or 25 deaths per year (Eck 2005; World Bank forthcoming). As a result, we are often faced with conflicting findings. Moreover, in many civil wars it is often hard to make a real distinction between deaths directly related to combat and deaths occurring indirectly as a result of war—either because of health and sanitary issues or because of other forms of violence related to the conflict (Lacina and Gleditsch 2005; Roberts 2006).[4]

Conflict mortality data disaggregated by gender are virtually nonexistent. None of the major institutions that collect conflict data has made systematic efforts to gather such data. From the little data available, we know that men are more likely to die during conflicts—if only because combatants are predominantly male. In addition, while recent studies have pointed to an overall decline in battle deaths, the female:male ratio of people dying as a direct effect of violent conflict seems to have gone up considerably in the post–Cold War era—that is, relatively more women are dying as a direct consequence of war (Ormhaug, Meier, and Hernes

---

2. Civilian deaths are usually considered "collateral damage" by the military. The problems related to collateral damage in Afghanistan—that is, civilian deaths caused by failed military attacks—have led to a number of innovations in NATO's data collection on civilian casualties. See Cameron, Spagat, and Hicks 2010.

3. The protocols for the collection of data often lack systematic definitions and hence are generally not consistent over time or across regions. While these data are important for quick impressions, it is hard to distill broader and more systematic lessons from them. Some observers have accused NGOs of grossly overreporting casualties, as the latest controversy on the Democratic Republic of the Congo illustrates.

4. War is often accompanied by other forms of violence, such as criminal and sexual violence. In addition, it must be pointed out that attendant fatalities related to disease, malnutrition, or exhaustion are often hard to quantify, in part because many countries lack reliable peacetime mortality data. See also Lacina and Gleditsch 2005; Roberts 2006.

2009; Lacina and Gleditsch 2005; Human Security Report Project 2005, 2010; Murray et al. 2002).

Some recent studies have also shown that the death rate of women is greater than that of men after the conflict is over (Ormhaug, Meier, and Hernes 2009). Thomas Plümper and Eric Neumayer (2006) have argued that the effect of war on women is particularly severe in ethnic conflicts. They also found that if in peacetime women are likely to outlive men, that difference in life expectancy becomes much smaller in conflict and post-conflict situations.[5]

Recent studies have also shown that women suffer more and die in proportionally greater numbers than do men from human rights abuses, the breakdown of social order, the lack of medical care, and the consequences of economic devastation. Some studies have argued that for women, the lawlessness of many post-conflict situations with their widespread violence is as dangerous and devastating as armed conflict itself (Ghobarah, Huth, and Russett 2003; for a different view, see Li and Wen 2005). It is obvious that the threat and fear of abuse in a post-conflict situation will keep women from leaving their homes, working, or otherwise participating in society. The reluctance to send children to school is usually an early indicator warning of widespread problems and lack of security. In Afghanistan, this is a grave problem with regard to girls' schools.

The destruction of infrastructures such as hospitals and schools causes great harm to family welfare and has a devastating effect on women and children. The desolation of the countryside and the presence of undetected mines make planting and harvesting very hazardous—and in many societies it is mainly the women who carry out these tasks. The lack of employment opportunities often has a greater direct effect on men, perhaps leading them into criminal activities, which in turn affect their families and communities.

The importance of collecting and analyzing conflict data was recognized by the members of the UN Security Council when adopting UNSCR 1325. Indeed, data on casualties and the causes of death would provide policymakers with great insights into the origins of violent conflict and when, where, and how to prioritize interventions. Unfortunately, much remains to be done in this area. For example, a report published by the United Nations in the fall of 2009 never mentions age and gender when discussing civilian protection policies (Holt, Taylor, and Kelly 2009). The absence of such data greatly impedes putting into place effective protection policies.

---

5. Plümper and Neumayer found that gender differences in life expectancy seem unaffected by interstate wars.

Women and War: In the Field

UNSCR 1325 describes women and children as "the vast majority of those adversely affected by armed conflict, including as refugees and internally displaced persons, and increasingly . . . targeted by combatants and armed elements[.]" Undersecretary-General John Holmes for the UN Office of the Coordination of Humanitarian Affairs (OCHA) stated in a 2009 briefing to the UN Security Council: "However familiar the challenges to the protection of civilians are[,] . . . ensuring that we respond to them in a comprehensive and consistent way continues to elude us" (Holmes 2009, 6).

The lawlessness and lack of protection are especially striking in refugee camps. Peacekeeping forces have also at times been the cause of much insecurity and have subjected local populations to sexual abuse. Finally, ensuring protection and equal participation requires that gender issues be taken into account when dealing with reforms of the security sector in the post-conflict phase.

Refugee and IDP Camps

Around the world, 42 million people have been forced from their homes. Of these, 15.2 million are refugees and 26 million are internally displaced persons (IDPs). Women and children make up 68 percent of refugees and 70 percent of IDPs, yet refugee camps are quite often run by male refugees and male humanitarian workers (UNHCR 2009). The camps, despite all efforts by the UN High Commissioner for Refugees and despite the organization's greatly improved gender strategies, are often very violent places. They are fortresses that still serve to protect warring groups, and the UNHCR rarely has at its disposal the security forces necessary to remove the combatants. There is a great shortage of nonmilitary security personnel in general, and in the camps in particular. Consequently, rapes occur at an alarming rate inside the camps. According to the UNHCR, there is a strong link between falling levels of assistance to refugees and their increasing vulnerability and exposure to forced sex work and sexual exploitation (UNHCR 2008). Refugee women rarely have any control over the distribution of food, blankets, health services, and other resources, and they must pay dearly for this dependence as they struggle for life's necessities for themselves and their children.

The security conditions in refugee camps would improve if both staff and policymakers would take a greater number of women into their ranks, and if the existing codes of conduct for all international staff were more strictly enforced. Refugee women need to be included in making decisions that affect them and their children's lives, the gender awareness of international personnel must be improved, and refugees must be given legal and political status. Many refugees, especially girls and women, have no identity cards and few are registered. Their redress is minimal and their legal status at times uncertain, even though the UNHCR has increasingly addressed these problems (UNHCR 2008).

Peacekeeping Operations

Allegations and revelations of sexual abuse by UN peacekeepers go back to the early 1990s and the peace operations in Cambodia and the Balkans. However, it is only in 2005, after the publication of a report on sexual abuse by UN peacekeepers in the Democratic Republic of Congo (DRC), that the United Nations started to address this problem more seriously. In addressing abuses, particularly sexual abuses by peacekeeping forces, the most important instruments have been so-called mainstreaming processes—namely efforts to increase gender sensitivity and consciousness on the part of male peacekeeping and security personnel through gender training and efforts to integrate and recruit women into peacekeeping operations and security forces. The thinking underlying these efforts mirrors standard democratic thought about the positive effects of representation and participation in decision making by those whose interests are affected, in this case women. This underlying assumption is also expressed in the opening paragraphs of UNSCR 1325.

Countries differ widely in the representation of women in their legislatures and in their commitment to gender equality. Many of those that have adopted gender equality policies also as a matter of policy recruit women into the security forces (Schjølset 2010). These policies make a case for acknowledging women's legitimate claim to participate and be represented in any type of peace operation, peacebuilding, and peace negotiation, as well as their right to security and to protection on par with men.

The active recruitment of women into the security forces is usually justified by appeals to gender equality and women's right of access to all types of positions in society, often supplemented by arguments of efficiency, utility, and complementary gender roles. The presence of women and creating a gender balance are viewed by many officers as salutary for their organization and for the success of the mission as a whole. Such justifications have increased with the greater number of humanitarian interventions and the increased contact of intervention forces with civilian populations. In the opinion of many officers, the presence of female colleagues in their teams has become mandatory if they are to effectively communicate with the civilian population—that is, with women as well as men. The U.S. Marines have deployed "female engagement teams" in Afghanistan in order to reach local women when units are out on patrol (Bumiller 2010). Norwegian

officers and those from other International Security Assistance Force
units deploy their female troops with the same aim in mind. Many observers claim that the participation of women among personnel deployed
in the security sector has proven to be crucial in bringing about successful
operations and in preventing criminal behavior. This is especially true of
all-female formed police units, such as the Indian one in Liberia, or the
Ghanaian and Nigerian women deployed in Sierra Leone (Carvajal 2010).
The Department of Peacekeeping Operations (DPKO) Gender Unit plans
to carry out an evaluation of the impact of women's participation in
peacekeeping operations during the past decade.[6]

Some experts have suggested that the presence of women in these
organizations enhances civilian women's access to services, that women
are more likely to enter into a dialogue rather than a confrontation with
the civilian population, that they help reduce sexual misconduct by male
international personnel, and that they enhance the confidence and trust of
civilians in general. Thus, according to most military leaders and political
decision makers, the implications of integrating women into both international and national security forces are wide-ranging and positive (Conaway
and Shoemaker 2008).

That said, more research is needed to evaluate the precise effects of
women's presence in the field. The anecdotal experience of those who have
deployed women in peacekeeping forces, in police forces, and among civilian personnel in peace operations is worth noting. Indeed, the actual
number of women involved in peace operations is still very small: in 2008,
women comprised 2 percent (1,700) of all troops, 3 percent (89) of military observers, and 7 percent of all police (Center on International Cooperation 2009). The numbers change radically when civilians are taken into
account. Thirty percent of all international civilian staff are women; 38
percent among the staff of the UN Department of Field Support are
women; and 30 percent of the professional staff at DPKO headquarters
are women. The uniformed personnel among the international and national
staff in the United Nations include 7,700 women (7 percent of the total).
However, only a small number fall into what might be considered the security sector. An exception is Liberia, where women made up 6 percent of
the military observers, 2 percent of the troops, and 18 percent of the police,
as well as 34 percent of the international civilian staff. These relatively
high numbers result from a conscious decision by the Liberian government and the United Nations to recruit women. Even more impressive,

---

6. Clare Hutchinson, gender adviser at UN DPKO, personal communication to Helga Hernes,
New York, April 2010.

the successful deployment of the female security personnel led to a 30 percent increase in the number of women in the national Liberian police force. A similar increase in the number of female police officers had earlier been observed in Kosovo, similarly as a result of the international deployment of women. The United Nations has made recruitment of police, including women, one of its top priorities, and aims to increase the proportion of female police officers to 20 percent by 2015. This initiative in part reflects the recognition that many contemporary security challenges, especially in countries recovering from conflict, are handled better by police than by military forces. In addition, in many post-conflict situations women's trust in all uniformed men is low, and they are reluctant to turn to male uniformed personnel for assistance.

The four countries contributing the most women soldiers to UN forces are Nigeria, India, Nepal, and Bangladesh. In most countries the number of available women professionals in the security sector is still very low, and for that reason the Norwegian and the Swedish governments have put great stress on recruiting women to their civilian crisis response units, which draw on individuals from all professions relevant to the security sector. This Scandinavian emphasis recognizes the ever-increasing need for personnel serving abroad who can communicate with both men and women, especially those women who are victims of sexual and gender-based violence, as well as the positive effects of female personnel in the field in peace operations. UNSCR 1325 aims to ensure women's right to representation and participation in all processes that affect their lives, including all types of peace operations, which—whether military, police, or civilian—are crucial for the effectiveness of the establishment of peace, stability, and security. The UN Police Division recognizes that there are still many obstacles to women's participation in the police service. Difficulties in recruitment, promotion, and retention are due in part to discrimination, and in part to the lack of any kind of satisfactory family policies, which not surprisingly affects women more than men (Police Division, OROLSI, DPKO 2010).

The major obstacle, however, is that countries contributing troops and police have few women in the ranks of their security personnel; they are not very successful at retaining or promoting the women whom they do recruit. Therefore, the prospects of recruiting significant numbers of women for future peacekeeping operations and meeting the demands of the United Nations are not optimistic. The recruitment and retention of female personnel in the security sector will for a period require affirmative action and antidiscrimination policies, as well as respect for women's need for health policies different from those of men and an end to sexual harassment, which still is a feature of all armies and police forces. What is needed, in other words, are policies and programs aimed at ensuring gender equality for all security forces, regardless of country of origin (Conaway and Shoemaker 2008).

As important as the presence and integration of women professionals is the training of men in what has come to be called "gender sensitivity." We know from experience that "gender blindness" is pervasive in male-dominated organizations, especially those that make up the security sector. Their organizational ethos is very masculine, and it is easier, for example, to speak about "zero-tolerance policies" or gender balance and percentages than to explain what equity or gender mainstreaming actually entails. Gender sensitivity is first of all an awareness of the basic human rights of women, which requires treating those who commit sexual transgressions as criminals and putting an end to their impunity. It is also the realization that in many situations women and men have different needs as well as different perceptions. It is a sad fact of life that many men tend to downplay other men's sexual transgressions and harassment of women, not realizing how such actions are experienced by women. Security forces need to be trained to respect women's equal worth as human beings, which among other things entails preventing and responding to violence against women. Only then can trust in the system, so often sorely lacking in post-conflict societies, begin to develop.

Security Sector Reform

The 1998 study commissioned by the Organization for Economic Cooperation and Development's Development Assistance Committee, titled *DAC Guidelines on Conflict, Peace and Development Cooperation,* marked the development community's willingness to address internal security issues after several decades of refusing to do so (Bryden 2007) and was an important step forward, since it changed the rules on the use of DAC's financial resources. Security sector reform became the natural extension of disarmament, demobilization, and reintegration programs.

The security sector encompasses military and paramilitary forces, police forces, border guards, customs services, and the judicial and penal system, and its reform is a decisive step toward closing the security gap. Reform of the security sector is not limited to security in the narrow sense of the term but instead, and more importantly, is concerned with the legitimacy of the state, as well as accountability, democracy, good governance, and the social contract between the citizen and the state. The core elements of security sector reform are strengthening the rule of law, the judicial system, and democratic institutions; combating organized crime; and putting an end to trafficking in small arms, light weapons, and persons.

The need to integrate gender concerns into these security reform efforts has now been recognized and accepted by most international actors. That said, despite efforts by organizations such as the Geneva Centre for the Democratic Control of Armed Forces (DCAF), which developed gender and security sector reform "tool kits" that are aimed at training security personnel (DCAF 2010), the resources at hand remain limited and the will to act is often lacking. Threats against men's security are generally taken more seriously by national and international authorities than threats to which women are exposed. Louise Olsson (2009) has coined the term "security equality" to describe women's equal right to protection from physical violence, a right often overlooked in peace settlements because women are absent from the negotiations. Personal safety and security and a firmly established rule of law are preconditions for women's participation in the labor market and in public life, and their participation in both arenas is essential if they are to become equal partners in the social and economic life of their societies. Security sector reform increases stability and trust in the rule of law, which are necessary for peacebuilding. Women's trust will depend on the system's ability to remove threats to their personal security.

UNSCR 1325 has provided important impetuses to introduce gender concerns into policies and practices that deal with the causes and consequences of violent conflict—some progress has been made, but too often gender concerns remain "ad-hoc, dependent of a few committed individuals or small-scale units. Women are still an afterthought in many instances— . . . the feel-good project to make donors and diplomats look good. A box to be ticked, a meeting to be had, a paragraph to be written" (Anderlini 2007, 230).

The Road Ahead

This volume examines some of the concerns that led to the adoption of UNSCR 1325 and takes stock of current thinking and understanding of the resolution's two pillars—power and protection. We examine what has been done thus far to ensure greater participation of women at the negotiating table as well as their participation in national prevention and post-conflict reconstruction strategies. We also examine the issue of sexual violence and discuss efforts to guarantee the protection of vulnerable groups, women in particular.

In chapter 2, Sanam Anderlini explores the impact of UNSCR 1325 in the legal sphere of power and protection, focusing on instances in which the resolution has contributed to the development of laws and practices at the international, national, and local levels. The chapter also discusses the resolution's implications for future programming related to the rule of law. Chapters 3 and 4 focus on the problem of protecting women in the context of war. Elisabeth Jean Wood examines the variations of sexual violence that occur in different conflicts. She argues that the internal dynamics of armed groups explain this variation and develops policy recommendations. Inger Skjelsbæk further addresses the complexity of wartime sexual violence by drawing on studies from wars in the former Yugoslavia to map what we know about sexual violence in war and how we should expand research strategies to help us understand and hence address this issue more effectively in the future.

In chapter 5, Tilman Brück and Marc Vothknecht shed light on the economic situation of women in post-conflict settings by analyzing recent evidence from both qualitative and quantitative research. The authors find the cessation of violence, as well as equal access to resources, education, training, and employment, to be key to women's economic empowerment in post-conflict societies. In the volume's conclusion, chapter 6, Donald Steinberg issues a call to action in order to realize the promise of UNSCR 1325. Steinberg suggests that the success of these efforts will be measured not by the number of resolutions passed or the amount of money spent, but by the progress made in protecting the lives of women on the ground and the opportunities to play their rightful and vital role in peace processes and post-conflict governments and economies.

UNSCR 1325 has been a major instrument for advancing the power of women or, put differently, the rights of women—rights to speak, rights to move freely, and rights to own. It also was a major impetus for paying greater attention to the protection of women, particularly their protection from sexual abuse. But at the operational level, the implementation of UNSCR 1325 remains limited to a few countries. Only 19 out of 192 countries have adopted national action plans, and their scope varies widely.[7] Similarly, at the United Nations, implementation of UNSCR 1325, be it in terms of gender balancing or of gender mainstreaming, remains a distant goal. The number of women appointed in high-level positions in peace and security operations remains extremely low—in 2008, out of sixty-six top management positions in peacebuilding only six were occupied by women (Puechguirbal 2010; WIIS 2006). Gender mainstreaming likewise remains far from complete. UN insiders as well as outside observers have pointed to a lack of understanding of what gender mainstreaming actually means, and they have noted the institution's lack of interest in pursuing it

---

7. In October 2010, the United States announced it would develop a National Action Plan.

seriously. At best, gender mainstreaming is viewed as a nonpolitical task. A recent analysis of UN documents concludes that most of them use stereotypical language that denies active roles for women and instead represents women mainly as victims (Puechguirbal 2010). In addition, women are persistently associated with children and cast as caretakers—portrayals that restrict them to the private sphere. Gender hierarchies are almost always taken as a given and women are most frequently "depicted as harmless victims in need of protection by male protectors" (Puechguirbal 2010, 177), leaving little room for women as independent agents. UN documents also tend to perpetuate the myth that women are somehow more peaceful than men.

In sum, despite the increased awareness at the policy level of how gender concerns affect international peace and security, implementation of gender sensitive policies is still flawed. Recent peacebuilding operations and interventions suggest that gender reforms do not necessarily strengthen the rights of women in a sustainable way (Bernard et al. 2008; Porter 2007). If women's particular human rights and concerns are not explicitly integrated into peacebuilding mandates, strategies, and plans, then women's concerns will continue to be marginalized and treated as matters that can be attended to later. Given the disproportionate exposure of women to violence in the wake of conflict, significant steps need to be taken to protect women, and to give them a stronger voice and greater visibility so that they are able to represent their own interests and participate in the reconstruction of their societies.

In 2000, members of the Security Council professed their belief that women play an important role in preventing and resolving conflicts and in peacebuilding and expressed the need to therefore provide women with the power to fully participate in making decisions about conflict prevention and resolution. World leaders also recognized that the continual assaults on women, particularly sexual assaults, have greatly hampered efforts at achieving durable peace and reconciliation—hence the importance of putting protective measures into place. The first decade of UNSCR 1325 has seen some progress, but women still lack power and are not given sufficient protection in contemporary wars.

Finally, we believe that it is important to engage the international relations field not only at an epistemological and ontological level but also on a well-grounded empirical level. By highlighting the relationship between micro-level local practices and macro-level global policies, we can lay bare the local impacts of global norms, practices, and regulations and discover how they affect local and global gender inequalities (True 2002; Youngs 2004; Tickner 2001; Enloe 2000; Goldstein 2003). In so doing we make possible a better understanding of the forces leading to war and peace. The lack of accurate data about how gender affects issues of power and inequality helps sustain many of the myths surrounding men and women and reinforces stereotypes.

References

Afshar, H., and D. Eade, eds. 2003. *Development, Women, and War: Feminist Perspectives.* Bloomfield, CT: Kumarian Press.

Anderlini, S. N. 2007. *Women Building Peace: What They Do, Why It Matters.* Boulder, CO: Lynne Rienner Publishers.

Baksh-Sodeen, R., ed. 2005. *Gender Mainstreaming in Conflict Transformation.* London: Commonwealth Secretariat.

Bernard, C., S. Jones, O. Oliker, C. Quantic Thurston, B. K. Stearns, and K. Cordell. 2008. *Women and Nation-Building.* Santa Monica, CA: RAND Corporation.

Bouta, T., and G. Frerks. 2002. "Women's Roles in Conflict Prevention, Conflict Resolution, and Post-Conflict Reconstruction: Literature Review and Institutional Analysis." Netherlands Institute of International Relation.

Bouta, T., G. Frerks, and I. Bannon. 2004. *Gender, Conflict, and Development.* Washington, DC: World Bank.

Bryden, A. 2007. "From Policy to Practice: The OECD's Evolving Role in Security System Reform." Policy Paper No. 22. Geneva Centre for the Democratic Control of Armed Forces (DECAF), Geneva.

Bumiller, E. 2010. "Letting Women Reach Women in Afghan War." *New York Times,* 6 March.

Cameron, E., M. Spagat, and M. Hicks. 2010. "Tracking Civilian Casualties under COMISAF's Tactical Directive." *British Army Review,* March, 32–38.

Carvajal, D. 2010. "A Female Approach to Peacekeeping." *New York Times,* 6 March.

Center on International Cooperation. 2009. *Annual Review of Global Peace Operations.* Boulder, CO: Lynn Rienner Publishers.

Conaway, C. P., and J. Shoemaker. 2008. "Women in United Nations Peace Operations: Increasing the Leadership Opportunity." Paper presented at Women in International Security, Georgetown University, Washington, DC, July.

DCAF. 2010. "Gender and Security Sector Reform Training Resource Website." Geneva Centre for the Democratic Control of Armed Forces (DCAF). Available at www.gssrtraining.ch (accessed 3 May 2010).

Eck, K. 2005. *A Beginner's Guide to Conflict Data: Finding and Using the Right Dataset.* UCDP Papers 1. Uppsala: Uppsala Conflict Data Program.

Enloe, C. 2000. *Maneuvers: The International Politics of Militarizing Women's Lives.* Berkeley: University of California Press.

Ghobarah, H., P. Huth, and B. Russett. 2003. "Civil Wars Kill and Maim People— Long After the Shooting Stops." *American Political Science Review* 97: 189–202.

Goldstein, J. S. 2003. *War and Gender: How Gender Shapes the War System and Vice Versa.* Cambridge: Cambridge University Press.

Greenberg, M. E., and E. Zuckerman. 2006. "The Gender Dimensions of Post-Conflict Reconstruction: The Challenges in Development Aid." UNU-WIDER Research Paper 2006/62. Available at www.responsibilitytoprotect.org/files/rp2006-62.pdf (accessed 28 June 2010).

Hassan, P. 2010. "The Afghan Peace Jirga: Ensuring That Women Are at the Peace Table." *USIP Peacebrief* 29, May.

Holmes, J. 2009. "Statement to Security Council on the Protection of Civilians in Armed Conflict." 14 January. Available at http://ochaonline.un.org/OCHAHome/AboutUs/TheUSGERC/2010StatementsandSpeeches/2009StatementsandSpeeches/tabid/5959/language/en-US/Default.aspx (accessed 3 May 2010).

Holt, V., G. Taylor, and M. Kelly. 2009. *Protecting Civilians in the Context of UN Peacekeeping Operations: Successes, Setbacks and Remaining Challenges.* Independent Study Jointly Commissioned by the Department of Peacekeeping Operations and the Office for the Coordination of Humanitarian Affairs. New York: United Nations.

Human Security Report Project. 2010. *The Shrinking Costs of War.* Part 2 of the *Human Security Report 2009.* Vancouver: HSRP.

Kumar, K., ed. 2001. *Women and Civil War: Impact, Organizations, and Action.* Boulder, CO: Lynne Rienner Publishers.

Lacina, B., and N. P. Gleditsch. 2005. "Monitoring Trends in Global Combat." *European Journal of Population* 21:145–66.

Li, Q., and M. Wen. 2005. "The Immediate and Lingering Effects of Armed Conflict on Adult Mortality: A Time Series, Cross-National Analysis." *Journal of Peace Research* 42:471–92.

Mazurana, D., A. Raven-Roberts, and J. Parpart, eds. 2005. *Gender, Conflict, and Peacekeeping.* Lanham, MD: Rowman and Littlefield.

Meintjes, S., M. Turshen, and A. Pillay, eds. 2002. *The Aftermath: Women in Post-Conflict Transformation.* London: Zed Books.

Moser, C. O. N., and F. Clark, eds. 2001. *Victims, Perpetrators, or Actors? Gender, Armed Conflict, and Political Violence.* London: Zed Books.

Murray, C., G. King, A. Lopez, N. Tomijima, and E. G. Krug. 2002. "Armed Conflict as a Public Health Problem." *British Medical Journal* 239:346–49.

Olsson, L. 2009. *Gender Equality and United Nations Peace Operations in Timor Leste.* Leiden: Martinus Nijhoff Publishers.

Ormhaug, C. M., P. Meier, and H. Hernes. 2009. *Armed Conflict Deaths Disaggregated by Gender.* PRIO Paper, 23 November. A Report for the Norwegian Ministry of Foreign Affairs. Oslo: International Peace Research Institute.

Plümper, T., and E. Neumayer. 2006. "The Unequal Burden of War: The Effect of Armed Conflict on the Gender Gap in Life Expectancy." *International Organization* 60:723–54.

Police Division, OROLSI, DPKO. 2010. "Gender and Police: Factsheet." April, United Nations, New York.

Porter, E. 2007. *Peacebuilding: Women in International Perspective.* London: Routledge.

Puechguirbal, N. 2010. "Discourses on Gender, Patriarchy and Resolution 1325: A Textual Analysis of UN Documents." *International Peacekeeping* 17:172–87.

Roberts, D. 2006. "Human Security or Human Insecurity? Moving the Debate Forward." *Security Dialogue* 37:249–61.

Sarosi, D. 2007. "Human Security: Does Gender Matter?" Paper presented at conference "Mainstreaming Human Security: The Asian Contribution," Bangkok, 4–5 October. Available at http://humansecurityconf.polsci.chula.ac.th/Documents/Presentations/Diana.pdf (accessed 28 June 2010).

Schjølset, A. 2010. "Closing the Gender Gap in the Armed Forces: The Varying Success of Recruitment and Retention Strategies in NATO." PRIO Policy Brief 4. Peace Research Institute Oslo, Oslo.

Tickner, J. A. 2001. *Gendering World Politics: Issues and Approaches in the Post–Cold War Era*. International Relations Series. New York: Columbia University Press.

True, J. 2002. "Engendering International Relations: What Difference Does Second-Generation Feminism Make?" Working Paper 2002/1, May. Department of International Relations, Australian National University, Canberra.

United Nations High Commissioner for Refugees (UNHCR). 2008. *UNHCR Handbook for the Protection of Women and Girls*. Geneva: UNHCR.

United Nations High Commissioner for Refugees (UNHCR). 2009. "Demographic Characteristics and Location." Chapter 5 in *UNHCR Statistical Yearbook 2008*, 51–56. Geneva: UNHCR. Available at www.unhcr.org/4bcc5aec9.html (accessed 3 May 2010).

WIIS. 2006. "United Nations Reform: Improving Peace Operations by Advancing the Role of Women." Washington, DC: Women in International Security.

Willett, S. 2010. "Introduction: Security Council Resolution 1325: Assessing the Impact on Women, Peace and Security." *International Peacekeeping* 17:142–58.

World Bank. Forthcoming. "Review of Databases on Violence and Conflict."

Youngs, G. 2004. "Feminist International Relations: A Contradiction in Terms? Or: Why Women and Gender Are Essential to Understanding the World 'We' Live In." *International Affairs* 80:75–87.

Zuckerman, E., and M. Greenberg. 2004. "The Gender Dimensions of Post-Conflict Reconstruction: An Analytical Framework for Policymakers." *Gender and Development* 12:70–82.

2

Translating Global Agreement into National and Local Commitments

Sanam Anderlini

W ith the demise of the Soviet Union in 1991 and the end of an era dominated by two superpowers, the nature of warfare began to shift over the course of the 1990s. The rise in intrastate conflicts and bitter manipulations of ethnicity was starkly evident in both Bosnia and Rwanda. In Latin America, the decline in Soviet patronage had given rise to narco-guerrillas, while in West Africa, particularly Sierra Leone and Liberia, the lines between soldiers and rebels were obscured, resulting in systemic acts of terror against civilian populations. The impact of this changing warfare on women was similar across conflict zones. Sexual violence, abductions for sexual slavery and for fighting, and forced displacement were emerging as key tactics of the new wars. The deliberate targeting of civilians was already notable. It was also evident that as the social fabric and trust within communities and families were destroyed, the tasks of building peace and promoting reconciliation would become more complex and nuanced. Simultaneously, however, in many conflict areas, women were emerging as voices of peace, mobilizing across communities, and using their social roles and networks to mitigate violence and mediate peace. Women wanted protection, but they also wanted to have their say in the resolution of conflict. They wanted the world community to acknowledge and include them in decision making about peace and security.

In 1999, International Alert, a British non-governmental organization (NGO), initiated a campaign focused on protecting women from the violence of war, as well as advocating for their participation in making decisions pertaining to peace and security. The campaign by the name of "Women Building Peace: From the Village Council to the Negotiating Table" was launched at the Hague Appeal for Peace Conference and sought support through a postcard campaign to change international policies pertaining to women, peace, and security.

Initially, three institutions were targeted: the European Parliament, the Organization for Economic Cooperation and Development (OECD), and the UN Security Council. As the campaign gained momentum, civil society organizations (CSOs) forged strategic alliances with other actors. Within the UN system, the United Nations Development Fund for Women (UNIFEM) became a key ally and conduit for reaching member-states within the Security Council, notably Bangladesh. In March 2000, Bangladesh first introduced to the council the theme of what would eventually become Resolution 1325. Following this successful step, CSO campaigners reached out to the Namibian government, identifying common ground shared by the demands of the campaign and the May 2000 Windhoek Declaration that had emerged from the international seminar "Mainstreaming a Gender Perspective in Multidimensional Peace Support Operations," cohosted by the UN Department of Peacekeeping Operations and the Namibian government. Namibia's willingness to partner with civil society and champion the cause alongside Bangladesh and Jamaica (also on the Security Council at the time) set the stage for a women's peace and security resolution based on four key pillars: conflict prevention, women's participation in decision making, protection of women's rights, and gender-sensitive peacekeeping. The passage of UN Security Council Resolution 1325 in October 2000 was swiftly followed by similar resolutions at the OECD and the European Parliament. By December 2000, a new normative framework had emerged.

The Security Council resolution was the most significant of the three, as it had global resonance and implications. Nonetheless, as is true of most international and diplomatic matters, there was ambiguity. On the one hand, as stated in Article 25 of the UN Charter, "The Members of the United Nations agree to accept and carry out the decisions of the Security Council in accordance with the present Charter." On the other hand, passage of this resolution—like countless other resolutions—under Chapter 6 of the UN Charter placed it into a legal limbo, as there was (and is) no penalty for noncompliance.

Moreover, unlike other thematic resolutions focusing on specific vulnerable target groups such as child combatants and demanding that attention be paid to their needs, UNSCR 1325 called for recognition of women's agency as peacemakers and their inclusion in peace processes. It was not just about recognizing women's victimization and need for fair treatment, it was a demand for establishing women as equal voices in making decisions pertaining to peace, security, and ultimately power. This represented a fundamental shift away from business as usual, in which parties to conflict or war, not parties to peace, are brought to the negotiation table. Needless to say, resistance to the inclusion of women, particularly women in civil society, was and remains profound.

Yet over the years, with increased understanding of the impact of warfare on civilians, women's continued advocacy, and the subsequent passage of Resolution 1820 (in 2008), Resolution 1888 (in 2009), and Resolution 1889 (in 2009), the normative framework has expanded considerably. The rhetoric addressing women's protection and calling for their inclusion in decision making has been strengthened (1889). Policy frameworks and advocacy campaigns have also been developed. But additional measures are needed to turn the rhetoric into reality in the lives of women most at risk. Linking the provisions of the resolutions to legal instruments and the rule of law is an important step in that direction.

Focusing on examples and developments at the international, national, and local levels, this chapter explores the impact of UNSCR 1325 in the legal sphere over the past decade and its future implications, including for programming related to the rule of law. The discussion is neither definitive nor comprehensive, given that the resolution covers a wide range of issues and the "rule of law"[1] is a principle of governance that applies to every sector. Instead, the chapter highlights instances in which the resolution has contributed to the evolution of international and national laws and practices. While analyzing the past, it also looks to the future and for ways in which the words and spirit of UNSCR 1325 could be better realized.

Impact and Implications on the International Level

Internationally, UNSCR 1325 has prompted significant work across a wide range of issues. But the resolution itself did not emerge in a vacuum. Not only was it a product of its time, but its provisions were influenced by real-time developments in other spheres. The section below focuses on

---

1. The United Nations defines "rule of law" as "a principle of governance in which all persons, institutions and entities, public and private, including the State itself, are accountable to laws" (UN Security Council 2004, 4).

three key areas: women's protection, sexual exploitation and abuse by peacekeepers, and women's participation in decision making.

Evolving Norms Regarding Sexual Violence

Advocates for the Security Council resolution drew substantively from the experiences and precedents set by the ad hoc tribunals of Rwanda and the former Yugoslavia, where women's rights advocates, particularly Balkan-based activists and the Women's Caucus for Gender Justice, had made their mark. As the former chief prosecutor of the International Criminal Tribunal for the Former Yugoslavia (ICTY), Richard Goldstone, recalled, if a woman had not been on the tribunal in the early years, there might not have been any indictments for gender-based crimes (Mertus and Van Wely 2004, 13).

As the ICTY was being formed, the key issue for the women's human rights movement was that rape be recognized as a direct violation of international law and a serious crime, not simply treated as a by-product of other crimes or a subset of "honor crimes." It was important that rape not be framed as an attack on personal dignity or honor and thus as less serious than physical harm, an approach that reinforces the notion of women as the property of men or their families, rather than as individuals with human rights (Mertus and Van Wely 2004, 17). They also pressed to extend the notion of liability for rape and sexual violence. Not only those who planned, ordered, and committed the act but also those who aided and abetted in planning, preparing, and executing the crime were liable. In addition, commanders who "knew or had reason to know" were liable. These provisions led to a number of landmark decisions that expanded "the understanding of sexual violence under international law" (Mertus and Van Wely 2004, 18–19).

In addition to placing rape and sexual assault firmly in the terrain of war crimes and crimes against humanity, the rules of procedure and evidence at the ICTY affected the protection of victims of sexual abuse. Rule 34 called for the creation of a victim's support unit to provide services and counseling to witnesses and victims, particularly those involved in sexual assault and rape cases. Specific mention was made of the need for qualified female staff to run the unit and for care to be made available for young dependents and accompanying persons, as well as relocation assistance for witnesses and flat fees to cover their costs incurred while away from home. Rule 96 provides that in cases of sexual assault, no corroboration of the victim's testimony is needed; consent given as a result of threats or coercion is not admissible by the defense, nor is the victim's prior sexual history. Other rules that benefited victims of sexual violence included maintaining the confidentiality of a victim's identity during investigations, permitting evidence to be submitted via deposition to spare victims and witnesses the difficulty of traveling to The Hague, and allowing the tribunal to take extra measures to protect the identity of witnesses and victims, such as sealing records, closing sessions, and using image- and voice-altering devices.

This precedent influenced the design of the International Criminal Court (ICC), which in turn was reinforced by UNSCR 1325. Key developments in the ICC statute include the recognition of rape, sexual slavery, enforced prostitution, pregnancy and sterilization, and other forms of sexual violence as crimes against humanity and war crimes. Trafficking is treated as slavery, and gender-based persecution is categorized as a crime against humanity. Institutional and procedural issues addressed in the Rome Statute establishing the ICC include witness protection programs (encompassing security and protective measures) and counseling through the creation of a victims and witness unit. The court can also award reparations, either as restitution, as compensation, or for rehabilitation.[2] Judges at the ICC are also required to have gender expertise—that is, knowledge of the differential implications of laws and procedures for women and men, and understanding of the issues that need to be addressed to ensure equitable treatment—and the balance of men and women among the staff and judges must be fair. Finally, states that ratify the ICC statute are required to amend their national laws, if necessary, to ensure conformity with its language. This is important, as national legislation criminalizing violence against women—when it even exists—is often lax or ineffective.

The ICC, with its limited jurisdiction, is of course not a panacea, but it has created new norms. These developments at the international level are slowly trickling down to the national level (see below). Efforts at preventing or prosecuting sexual and gender-based violence within countries remain limited. Nonetheless, the normative shift and progress between the mid-1990s and 2010 are noteworthy.

In less than two decades, the international community has moved from failing to recognize sexual and gender-based violence to mandating, in UNSCR 1325, that sexual violence be excluded from amnesty provisions to finally and unequivocally recognizing sexual violence as a threat to peace and security, with the passage of UNSCRs 1820 and 1888. They require that actions be taken to prevent, report, and prosecute such crimes. Other important developments are the formulation of indicators for reporting and the creation of a senior post dedicated to addressing sexual and gender-based violence. Although actual implementation of the resolutions' provisions mandating systematic care and support for victims and effective preventive measures is still largely lacking, the silence and

---

2. For more information about the workings of the court, see www.iccwomen.org (retrieved 26 July 2010).

invisibility that for so long has cloaked sexual violence in war are at last coming to an end.

Over the past decade, NGOs and other entities have published count-less reports and recommendations to minimize sexual and gender-based violence in conflict and emergency settings. The problems are complex, but the causes and consequences of sexual and gender-based violence can be tackled if the political will and resources are available. In the future, comprehensive approaches to sexual and gender-based violence might be prompted by making support to major humanitarian agencies receiving public funds (both from the United Nations and not) conditional on dem-onstrating systematic and strategic efforts to prevent and limit sexual and gender-based violence in refugee and internally displaced person camps, as well as during repatriation and rehabilitation efforts. In other words, just as humanitarian agencies have systems in place to limit and prevent hunger (a clear threat and a consequence of violence and displacement), they should develop and implement systems to prevent and limit sexual and gender-based violence (another known and common consequence of natural and man-made crises).

Basic compliance with existing guidelines, including those found in the Inter-Agency Standing Committee's "gender handbook in humanitarian action" (IASC 2006) on the protection of women, men, boys, and girls, could be an effective first step toward systematic prevention of sexual and gender-based violence. Better analysis of the sources and causes of such forms of violence might also suggest entry points for prevention. For ex-ample, if teenage girls are being abused by relatives or by "money men" (as in Liberia) who provide school funds in return for sex, then scholarships and school fee support could be provided to the most vulnerable. Increas-ing direct support to NGOs and CSOs providing care for victims and promoting prevention through education and programs raising awareness could also have an immediate impact. It is both cost-effective and a means of building local capacities.

Sexual Exploitation and Abuse

Peacekeepers' involvement in the sexual exploitation and abuse of local populations was not explicitly mentioned in UNSCR 1325, but the problem was alluded to. The resolution, like the Windhoek Declaration that served as one of its founding documents, calls for increased gender balance in peace operations, mentions the need to improve the training of peace-keepers in "gender and HIV/AIDS," and urges member-states to fund such training. The Windhoek Declaration had already noted the need for train-ing on a code of conduct, on the host country's cultural history and social norms, on sexual harassment and assault, and on the provisions of the

Convention on the Elimination of All Forms of Discrimination against Women (CEDAW).[3]

The references to gender issues, particularly sexual assault and HIV/AIDS, suggest that the UN system and member-states were already aware of pervasive sexual exploitation and abuse within the ranks of peacekeepers and civilian personnel. The 1991 UN peacekeeping mission to Cambodia, in particular, was known for its widespread sexual exploitation of desperately poor local populations, its spread of HIV/AIDS, and its promotion of prostitution (Featherston 1995; Defeis 2008). But the culture of tolerance of such behavior prevailed, despite the introduction of a "zero-tolerance" policy toward sexual exploitation and abuse in 2003. Nonetheless, the demand for more women in peace operations and for gender training for peacekeepers provided an avenue toward greater scrutiny of behavior during deployment.

The first UN report on sexual exploitation and abuse was published in 2002, and it led to the formation of an interagency task force that defined sexual exploitation and abuse and developed a code of conduct, which included a zero-tolerance policy. But abuses persisted, and in 2004, when news of yet more UN peacekeeping sex scandals broke, the institution was forced to take stronger measures. In 2005 the Department of Peacekeeping Operations (DPKO) established its Conduct and Discipline Unit (CDU), comprising teams that provide guidance to field missions, organize training sessions, and record allegations of misconduct.[4] Although initially the United Nations had the right to conduct investigations, a 2007 UN General Assembly resolution limited its role, stating that the United Nations can investigate only if countries are unable or unwilling to do so themselves.

Tensions have remained high. In 2008, the CDU launched its global misconduct tracking system database. Meanwhile, in October 2008, 180 civil society organizations signed an open letter urging the UN secretary-general to take more assertive leadership on the matter and requested that special representatives of the secretary-general—the senior-most representatives in UN missions—be made personally responsible for any violation and asked to resign if one should occur. The signers also demanded that UN personnel involved in sexual exploitation and abuse be brought to justice, including through the International Criminal Court mechanism.[5] But

---

3. The full text of CEDAW, together with additional information, is available at www.un.org/womenwatch/daw/cedaw/cedaw.htm.

4. For more information, see http://cdu.unlb.org/.

5. The petition was initiated at a conference at UNESCO in Paris celebrating the sixtieth anniversary of the Universal Declaration of Human Rights; Mouvement Mondiale de Meres collected the signatures. The secretary-general's office responded after five months but did not accept the key demands for special representatives of the secretary-generals' accountability or for bringing violators to justice.

member-states resisted. According to a 2010 report in the *Wall Street Journal*'s online edition, out of eighty-two requests for information on sexual exploitation and abuse from troop-contributing countries (TCCs), the United Nations received only fourteen responses. Too often, member-states drop cases, even when there is overwhelming evidence of wrongdoing. In one instance, a TCC claimed that its peacekeepers would not be safe on their return if the local communities knew that they had been accused of sexual crimes (Stecklow and Lauria 2010).

At the same time, after years of inertia, some progress has been made in deploying female peacekeepers. The Indian contingent of women peacekeepers in Liberia, though small, has had an overwhelmingly positive response. They have been effective role models and by many accounts more trusted by local populations. In a country plagued by sexual violence during and after a war, the presence of women security personnel provides a modicum of relief to victims (Basu 2010). As we look to the future, however, the question remains whether the United Nations will build and expand on this success by requesting and deploying more female personnel, or will carry on with business as usual.

Indeed, sexual exploitation and abuse by UN peacekeepers remains among the most contentious and bitter of issues. Although the United Nations itself has taken some steps to address the challenge, much more can be done. In the future, the UN member-states committed to ending sexual exploitation and abuse could take the following steps:

- Establish as a criterion for eligibility as a TCC that female participation in peacekeeping units must be at least 25 percent. The UN leadership and supportive member-states should exploit the fact that many countries rely on providing peacekeepers as an important source of revenue. If a quota of female peacekeepers is introduced, it would have multiple benefits: increased female personnel will enhance the United Nations' capacity to reach out and protect women in communities; women peacekeepers are unlikely to engage in sexual exploitation and abuse; and the presence of women in peacekeeping units will alter the environment and inhibit the behavior of their male colleagues.
- Vet former female combatants from Central America, South Africa, Nepal, and other countries and give them the opportunity to be trained and deployed as peacekeepers. Many of these women have the relevant skills and can easily be retrained.
- Give existing TCCs such as Sri Lanka and India support to establish academies for women so that they can be trained and prepared for careers in peacekeeping.

- Establish a "three strikes and you're out" rule: after three incidents of sexual exploitation and abuse were reported, countries would lose their eligibility for being a TCC.
- Set deadlines for TCCs to respond to cases of sexual exploitation and abuse. If there is no response, the cases in question could be automatically put into the United Nations' hands for investigation.
- Bolster the current team of investigators, which lacks the resources and personnel to cope with the cases now being brought forward.

Women's Participation

The call in UNSCR 1325 for increasing women's participation and the reference to "indigenous conflict resolution mechanisms" to prevent, resolve, and recover from conflict also builds on precedent. The experiences of the Guatemalan civic forum, the Northern Ireland Women's Coalition, and the South African transition, which afforded women equal representation in the negotiations process, inspired and informed the resolution. Yet despite these precedents and the variety of models available that might be adapted to other peace processes, it remains the area addressed by UNSCR 1325 where the least progress has been made. An analysis conducted by UNIFEM shows that women have constituted fewer than 7 percent of negotiators on official delegations in peace processes since 2000, and just under 3 percent of signatories. Most strikingly, in thirteen major comprehensive peace agreement processes since 2000, not one single woman was appointed as a mediator (UNIFEM 2009). Although UNSCR 1820 calls for women to be involved in national-level structures of peacebuilding and UNSCR 1889 demands even more forcefully their participation in all aspects of recovery, their inclusion continues to be ad hoc.

Within the UN system, the Department of Political Affairs (DPA) is the entity with primary responsibility for preventive diplomacy, peacemaking, and mediation. It also plays a pivotal role in keeping the Security Council informed and in determining where the council will undertake missions. In addition, DPA drafts the terms of reference (TORs) for missions and senior personnel, and is involved in selecting and recruiting envoys. It was also the first UN entity to undertake a department-wide process to build staff capacity and plan to implement the resolution. In 2006, DPA issued its department-wide action plan, endorsed by its leadership, that provided specific guidance on reporting and on consulting and engaging women in peace processes. But changes in its leaders and their persistent lack of support have hampered its efforts. It is further challenged by the failure of member-states to support it with funding and other resources.

The little progress that has been made can be credited in part to the demands made by CSOs in conflict countries and to UNIFEM's technical support. DPA's action plan and subsequent field office planning also raised staff awareness and increased the pressure on the department to act. By 2010, as the tenth anniversary of the resolution loomed and the U.S. administration took a more serious interest in the agenda, the Department's leadership was prodded into action. In May 2010, DPA and UNIFEM launched a joint strategy to promote female mediators, ensure that all mediation processes include advisers on gender, and enhance the capacities of women in CSOs to engage in peace processes. Without full financial support from member-states, however, the strategy will not become reality.

In addition to fully implementing the DPA/UNIFEM efforts, in the immediate term the UN Peacebuilding Commission, an intergovernmental body responsible for supporting peace efforts, could ensure that all its in-country processes fully include members of civil society, women, and peace groups and do not become just another vehicle for government officials to access funds. The United Nations could also establish parameters and the highest standards of practice by developing criteria for eligibility of participation (or, at minimum, systematic consultation) in peace processes that it mediates, endorses, and supports. Clearly, armed actors will continue to be engaged in an effort to win a cease-fire and end war. But the United Nations could determine standards and modalities for including nonviolent actors in the negotiations for peacebuilding and power sharing. Doing so would also press armed actors (who claim to represent communities) to be more transparent and accountable to the public regarding their views and priorities for recovery.

Moreover, the United Nations could use its influence to encourage member-states to abide by the same parameters when they mediate or facilitate talks, as follows:

- Groups that demonstrate a commitment to finding peaceful resolution to conflict—including those that offer creative alternative solutions to intractable conflicts and are committed to peacebuilding and the betterment of lives and communities affected by war—would be included into UN processes.
- Even if parties to conflict reject their inclusion at formal negotiations, the United Nations should consult with peace groups and bring their voices to the formal and informal venues where mediation is taking place.
- The United Nations should consult with peace groups, determine their key priorities and concerns, and then take these issues to armed actors and states to seek their responses and solutions. In other words, those

engaged in violence must be answerable to the demands of affected groups and communities.

These parameters would (a) send the message that violence alone is no longer the means of gaining international attention and/or legitimacy, (b) allow peace groups emerging from communities from which warring parties come to pressure those parties to reach a resolution and address the issues that concern the communities, and (c) help shift the agenda of negotiations away from a focus on cease-fires and power distribution to the substantive complex issues associated with peacebuilding, the needs of victims and communities, and comprehensive peace.

Actions at the National Level

Use and ownership of UNSCR 1325 at the national level have varied significantly across countries and over time. Immediately after it was adopted, the resolution was largely unknown, and funding to support its implementation was limited. Its promotion has largely been the work of CSOs working nationally and transnationally. They used (and continue to use) the resolution as an advocacy tool; some of the ways they seek to influence domestic policy and legislation through international laws and norms are described below.

UNSCR 1325 as a Tool at the National Level

From Kosovo to Kenya, women's groups have used the resolution to legitimate their demands for participation in decision making about peace and security, as well as to call for gender-sensitive policies and laws. They have had mixed results. In Kosovo, for example, CSOs faced resistance from the international community (Kosovo Women's Network 2009). Similarly, in Guinea-Bissau CSOs were excluded from the UN Peacebuilding Commission's national-level counterparts and advocated for inclusion with support from other UN entities.[6] In Kenya, on the other hand, during the post-election violence in 2008, women mobilized to mediate between conflicting groups in communities and cited UNSCR 1325 to justify their engagement.[7] In the Israeli-Palestinian conflict, drawing on the resolution, women from both sides joined together with female representatives of the Quartet to form the International Women's Commission (IWC). Despite its own internal struggles, the IWC has sought to provide analysis about

---

6. These issues were raised in a workshop that the author ran for the UN mission in Guinea-Bissau in April 2008.

7. Discussions with activists, Amman, Jordan, March 2010.

and solutions to the ongoing conflict with a unified voice. Yet its demands for inclusion in peace talks have been rebuffed.

A decade since its adoption, the resolution has enabled women to make some inroads into formal and governmental processes, but their fight remains an uphill struggle. That the international community has been resistant to their demands is an added blow. The least that women in conflict zones expect is that international actors—especially multilateral and regional entities—will themselves comply with the resolution.

Beyond advocacy, CSOs in some countries have worked with members of government to put UNSCR 1325 on the legislative agenda. The results are mixed.

- In the United States, Congresswoman Eddie Bernice Johnson introduced the principles and many provisions of the Security Council resolution into Congress in 2003. She succeeded in passing a congressional resolution on the subject, but it is not binding and has no means of implementation.
- In Israel, a coalition of women's groups in collaboration with Knesset members successfully passed legislation calling for the inclusion of women in all committees and decision-making bodies created to deal with national security and peace issues. Implementation of the law remains a challenge. Lack of transparency around membership in committees means that the selections are made before activists can demand enforcement of the laws. The demand for "women" has also opened up questions about which women, particularly in light of the marginalization of minorities in Israel.
- In Colombia, drawing on Resolution 1325, the Congreso passed legislation that led to two women from the women's peace movement outside government being named to the National Reconciliation and Reparations Commission.
- In Liberia, legislation and judicial reform pertaining to sexual and gender-based violence, particularly rape, are tied to the government's commitments to realizing UNSCR 1325. Nonetheless, given the limited capacities of the state's police and judiciary, implementation and application of the laws remain weak.

Despite its small scope, this approach can lay the foundations for comprehensive adoption of the resolution's provisions. It can also help dispel accusations of interference or the imposition of values from outside. Implementation of the laws does remain problematic, however.

National Action Plans

The provisions of the resolution are directed at specific actors, including UN member-states, but it included no call for national action plans (NAPs). Nonetheless, since 2005, largely because of advocacy from civil society and because momentum has built up within the UN system, a number of governments have begun to develop NAPs. Donor countries are integrating the issues into their foreign and development aid policy and practice. Developing and conflict-affected states such as Liberia are also devising NAPs that take into account their own context and priorities.

In principle, NAPs are a good start. If they are developed consultatively, the process itself is effective in raising awareness of the issues and challenges facing women. Commitments, when they are made, are a means of gaining traction and ownership at the national level. But typically NAPs are not legislated. They are policy documents, and thus can be ignored or altered with shifts in government interests and changes in power. Moreover, there is no penalty for noncompliance. In some instances, the NAPs are unfunded, making their implementation difficult.

As yet there is no systematic method promoted by the United Nations to assist governments in developing NAPs. Indeed, different UN entities (notably UNIFEM and the United Nations Population Fund, or UNFPA) are engaged in supporting governments in this task, with no consistency to their approaches. But as more countries take up the issues, the exchange of experiences, increased awareness, and ownership of the agenda will likely have a positive cumulative impact.

For countries adopting NAPs to implement UNSCR 1325, the link to legislation is important to ensure that the commitments do not disappear as governmental policy or leadership changes. In 2009 the Philippines adopted its NAP, which has a number of provisions with legislative implications.

Donor countries could legislate that gender sensitivity, particularly in conflict-affected countries, be a condition of development or recovery aid. In addition, countries that engage in mediation could also condition their support on the inclusion and representation of women's perspectives.

There is also an urgent need for government, foreign affairs, and military personnel to gain a more systemic awareness of UNSCR 1325's provisions (and a broader understanding of the gender dimensions of conflict, peace, and recovery processes). Integrating the issues into existing training programs and briefings could help enhance understanding and produce more systematic approaches.

Finally, the devil is largely in the details. All staff engaged in conflict prevention, resolution, and recovery must be required to demonstrate gender sensitivity as a condition of employment. The TORs of missions and envoys should explicitly call for consultation with, and the representation of, women in decision-making forums. There should be incentives to reach these goals, as well as penalties for staff noncompliance.

Normalizing 1325 at the Local and Provincial Level

It is rare for international norms to be being enacted at subnational levels. But the nature of conflict and its implications for women are such that often the most direct effects are felt at the local and provincial level. A key challenge is to determine effective ways of promoting awareness of, compliance with, and adaptation of the resolution to local contexts. A number of approaches are possible.

Inclusion of Women in Local Councils and in Village Forums and Decision-Making Bodies

In many settings, women are seeking to increase their representation in national legislatures and in local-level councils simultaneously. Opportunities at the local level at times show more promise. In Sri Lanka, for example, in 2002 a World Bank project focusing on the rehabilitation of irrigation systems in conflict-affected areas drew on mothers' networks to create women's village development councils parallel to the existing councils dominated by men. At first there was resistance from the men, but women's contributions to the community as a whole changed the dynamics of gender relations and won the men's respect (World Bank 2007). A further consequence was increased economic support for widows and women who did not benefit from the original irrigation program.

Similarly, in Rwanda, at the local or cell level, women's councils were also established in parallel to but connected with the local councils. In addition, 30 percent of the seats on provincial councils were reserved for women and the same proportion for youth (who voted on separate ballots). These structures provide openings for women to engage in decision making (Powley 2003).

In Kenya, women drew upon UNSCR 1325 to advocate for inclusion in local peace committees established by the government in the violent aftermath of the 2007 elections. Their ability and willingness to engage in dispute resolution, drawing on traditional social networks and methods, have helped overcome the recalcitrance and antipathy often evident among the male elites. They also succeeded in getting the Commission of Inquiry into

Post Election Violence to address sexual violence that occurred during the crisis (CIPEV 2008).[8]

Common Ground between Civil Law and Custom

In conflict-affected societies that lack a strong state, people usually rely on traditional and customary mechanisms to resolve disputes—a situation that can be profoundly challenging for women. On the one hand, customary systems of justice may discriminate against them. In particular, in many societies the stigma associated with victims of sexual and gender-based violence can be profound. Rape victims are sometimes forced by their own families to marry their rapist to restore the family honor; in other instances, victims can be driven out of their communities.

On the other hand, although civil procedures may be fairer in principle, in practice their effectiveness is limited due to the weakness of the state and its police. Liberia is a case in point. The rape laws and court dedicated to prosecuting sexual crimes are groundbreaking, but for most victims they remain inaccessible. Moreover, families' reliance on male breadwinners can often mean that victims are forced into silence or choose not to seek civil justice for fear that imprisoning the perpetrator will leave his family destitute.

But impunity comes at a high cost, as unchecked violence increases the tolerance of violence at the domestic level. It can also lead to vigilantism as families take on the task of revenge and retribution, thus perpetuating communal violence. In some instances, impunity for perpetrators can lead to the death of victims who are viewed as having shamed their clan or family.

The challenge therefore is to find opportunities for engaging with existing traditional systems and leaders to ensure that women receive fair treatment, and then to bring further awareness to both men and women where socio-cultural norms and practices perpetuate discrimination or condone sexual and gender-based violence.

Institutionalizing the core principles and provision of UNSCR 1325 at the local level has tremendous promise for making it a basic tenet of national rule of law. Perhaps surprisingly, rural areas and local communities are often more ready to accept changes in socio-cultural norms than are bureaucracies in capital cities. People—men and women—who have lived with the reality of war and experienced firsthand women's involvement and key contributions to peace are often more prepared than their urban counterparts to accept women in leadership and decision-making positions. But the issue must be approached from a ground-up perspective rather than

---

8. Kenyan women activists, discussions and correspondence with the author, March 2010.

with a top-down directive. Doing so requires two key steps. First, the resolution must be simplified and applied to local contexts and processes; and second, processes must be put in place to enable community stakeholders to analyze the impact of conflict on their lives, reflect on the relevance of the resolution to their situation, and identify priorities for action. For example, in Nepal in the immediate aftermath of the peace agreement in 2006, the UN system under the leadership of UNFPA took the following actions:

- Translation of the resolution.
- Production of a local language cartoon booklet describing the provisions of the resolution for policymakers.
- Provision of a one-page document linking the relevant provisions of UNSCR 1325 to key elements of the peace process.
- Support for a national street theater troop to convey through dance, drama, and music the experiences of women in conflict.
- Facilitation of workshops tailored to local and rural populations, informing them of the basic principles of the resolution and enabling them to determine priorities and means of implementation.

One-off actions will not be enough, however. An interactive process of consultation is needed, as a joint analysis of the problems and solutions can set the stage for local adoption of the resolution's provisions. Another approach, currently being developed by the Global Network of Women Peacebuilders, is to reach out to local governments and encourage them to pass legislation that mirrors and complies with the provisions of UNSCR 1325.

Similarly the International Civil Society Action Network (ICAN), in partnership with the Massachusetts Institute of Technology (MIT) Center for International Studies and a number of nationally based NGOs, is proposing a Women's Security Campaign. The aim is to strengthen women's networks in order to bring awareness and action on national security policymaking, and to establish direct partnerships with national security services (police and military) in order to uphold zero tolerance of sexual and gender-based violence.

Outreach to and partnership with elders, traditional leaders, and influential figures, particularly men, is integral to these initiatives. There is significant work under way by NGOs internationally to engage men as partners in the prevention of violence against women. They need to be developed and scaled up. Lessons need to be drawn from local culture and religion to root the aspirations of UNSCR 1325 in each context. For example, instead of assuming that rape is culturally condoned or cannot be punished, it might be reframed as a transgression of social taboos that requires taking punitive actions against perpetrators.

Dialogue and exploration of the issues can help defuse accusations that these are Western norms being introduced to threaten local ways of life. This is a delicate and complex area, requiring partnership with well-respected groups and individuals who have deep knowledge of local socio-cultural norms and the ability to frame issues in ways that are both acceptable and can garner the support of a wider cross section of leaders, while pushing the envelope to ensure sustained gains for women.

Conclusion

In 2010, the world continues to grapple with the challenges of violence. The majority of peace processes that delivered so-called peace have re-sulted in new forms of violence and insecurity including criminality, gangs, and higher rates of sexual and gender-based violence—a perpetual state of no war, no peace, that has detrimental effects on all aspects of po-litical, social, and economic development.

The nature of war and violence continues to change, and rising militarization is making peacebuilding ever more complex. In 2000, when women called for the adoption of UNSCR 1325, they were already experiencing these changes and understood that conducting business as usual would no longer suffice to promote sustainable positive peace. Inclusivity and attention to the gender dimensions of recovery and rehabilitation benefit not just women but society at large. Greater protection is also a means of reducing the cost of conflict. Lost lives and the economic impact of violence on every sector drain resources and human capital. Ironically, the focus on women has also led to greater attention to men. We are seeing more clearly the profound crises and pressures that confront them as well in times of conflict and violence.

The demand for participation seeks to draw on all existing capacities and stakeholders committed to peace. It wrests control away from the minority who use violence to further their ends and may have no real interest in fos-tering peace or democracy, which would lead to a reduction in their power. The agenda contained in UNSCR 1325 is an important tool to help shift the practice of international peace and security away from twentieth-century ap-proaches to more effective ways of addressing twenty-first-century problems. It is an urgent and necessary step toward finding more effective solutions.

References

Basu, M. 2010. "Indian Women Peacekeepers Hailed in Liberia." *CNN.com*, 2 March. Available at www.cnn.com/2010/WORLD/africa/03/02/liberia.women/index.html (accessed 28 June 2010).

Commission of Inquiry on Post Election Violence (CIPEV). 2008. *Report of the Commission of Inquiry on Post Election Violence.* Nairobi: CIPEV. Available at www.standard media.co.ke/downloads/Waki_Report.pdf (accessed 18 August 2010).

Defeis, E. 2008. "U.N. Peacekeepers and Sexual Abuse and Exploitation: An End to Impunity." *Washington University Global Studies Law Review* 7:185–214.

Featherston, A. B. 1995. "UN Peacekeepers and Cultures of Violence." *Cultural Survival Quarterly* 19.1, Spring. Available at www.culturalsurvival.org/publications/cultural-survival-quarterly/bosnia-and-herzegovina/un-peacekeepers-and-cultures-violenc (accessed July 2010).

Inter-Agency Standing Committee (IASC). 2006. *Women, Girls, Boys and Men: Different Needs—Equal Opportunities.* Available at www.humanitarianinfo.org/iasc/documents/ subsidi/tf_gender/IASC%20Gender%20Handbook%20%28Feb%202007%29. pdf (accessed 18 August 2010).

Kosovo Women's Network. 2009. *Monitoring Implementation of Resolution 1325 in Kosova.* 2nd ed. Prishtina: Kosovo Women's Network. Available at www.womensnet work.org/images/pdf/Monitoring%20Implementation%20of%20UNSCR%20 1325%20in%20Kosova.pdf (accessed 28 June 2010).

Mertus, J., with O. H. Van Wely. 2004. *Women's Participation in the International Criminal Tribunal for the Former Yugoslavia (ICTY): Transitional Justice for Bosnia and Herzegovina.* Women Waging Peace Commission, Hunt Alternatives Fund. Available at www.huntalternatives.org/download/19_women_s_participation_in_the_interna tional_criminal_tribunal_for_the_former_yugoslavia_icty_transitional_justice_for_ bosnia_and_herzegovina.pdf (accessed 28 June 2010).

Powley, E. 2003. *Strengthening Governance: The Role of Women in Rwanda's Transition.* Women Waging Peace Policy Commission, Hunt Alternatives Fund. Available at http://www.huntalternatives.org/pages/8095_strengthening_governance_the_role_ of_women_in_rwanda_s_transition.cfm (accessed 18 August 2010).

Stecklow, S., and J. Lauria. 2010. "U.N. Mum on Probes of Sex-Abuse Allegations." *Wall Street Journal* (online), 21 March. Available at http://online.wsj.com/article/SB1 0001424052748704188104575083334130312808.html (accessed 28 June 2010).

United Nations Development Fund for Women (UNIFEM). 2009. "Women's Participation in Peace Negotiations: Connections between Participation and Influence" April. Available at http://www.www.realizingrights.org/ . . . /UNIFEM_handout_Women_ in_peace_processes_Brief_April_20_2009.pdf (accessed 1 September 2010).

United Nations Security Council. 2004. "The Rule of Law and Transitional Justice in Conflict and Post-Conflict Societies." S/2004/616. 23 August. Available at http:// daccess-dds-ny.un.org/doc/UNDOC/GEN/N04/395/29/PDF/N0439529.pdf (accessed 28 August 2010).

World Bank. 2007. "Restarting Irrigation in Sri Lanka's Farming Zone." *IDA at Work,* May.

3

Rape Is Not Inevitable during War

Elisabeth Jean Wood

W hile sexual violence occurs in all wars, its extent varies dramatically. During the conflict in Bosnia-Herzegovina, the sexual abuse of Bosnian Muslim women by Bosnian Serb forces was so systematic and widespread that it was a crime against humanity under international law. In Rwanda, the widespread rape of Tutsi women comprised a form of genocide, according to the International Criminal Tribunal for Rwanda. In such settings, sexual violence frequently takes place in public, in front of family and community. Other cases include the janjaweed militias in Darfur, the Soviet and Japanese armies in World War II, and the various armed groups in the eastern Democratic Republic of Congo (DRC).[1] Yet sexual violence in some conflicts is remarkably limited despite other violence against civilians (Wood 2006, 2008a). Even in some cases of ethnic conflict, sexual violence is limited; the conflict in Israel/Palestine is an example. Some armed groups, such as the Salvadoran and Sri Lankan insurgencies, appear to effectively

1. This chapter was first published in *Collective Crimes and International Criminal Justice: An Interdisciplinary Approach*, ed. A. Smeulers and E. van Sliedregt (Antwerp: Intersentia, 2010). Reprinted with permission of the editors.

This chapter draws on Wood 2006, 2008a, and 2009. I am grateful for research support from the Harry Frank Guggenheim Foundation, the United States Institute of Peace, the MacMillan Center for International and Area Studies of Yale University, and the Santa Fe Institute, and for research assistance from Tess Lerner-Byars, Molly O'Grady, and Kai Thaler.

prohibit their combatants from engaging in sexual violence against civilians.

The form of sexual violence varies as well. In some conflicts, it takes the form of sexual slavery; in others, state agents engage in sexualized torture of persons suspected of collaborating with insurgents; in others, combatants target women of particular groups during ethnic or political cleansing; in still others, individuals engage in it opportunistically; and in some conflicts, all or nearly all forms occur. In some wars, only females are targeted; in others, males are as well. Some acts of wartime sexual violence are committed by individuals; many are committed by groups. Some acts occur in private settings; many are public, in front of family or community members.

In some settings, wartime sexual violence appears to magnify existing cultural practices; in others, patterns of sexual violence appear to be wartime innovations by armed groups. In some conflicts, the pattern of sexual violence is symmetric, with all parties to the war engaging in sexual violence to roughly the same extent. In other conflicts, it is very asymmetric as one armed group does not respond in kind to sexual violence by the other party. Sexual violence often increases over the course of the conflict; in some conflicts, it decreases. Sexual violence varies in extent and form among civil wars as well as interstate wars, among ethnic wars as well as nonethnic, and among secessionist conflicts (Wood 2006, 2008a, 2009). Despite the challenges to gathering data on this sensitive topic, the variation does not appear to be a product of inadequately reported violence: there are well-documented cases at the low end of the spectrum of sexual violence as well as the high end.

The observed variation is not explained by the dominant approaches in the literature on wartime sexual violence. With some exceptions, the literature focuses on cases where the pattern of sexual violence represents one end of the observed spectrum, namely, the widespread rape of civilian girls and women as in Bosnia, Rwanda, and Sierra Leone. Common explanations for wartime rape reflect that emphasis: Rape is an effective strategy of war, particularly of ethnic cleansing; rape is one form of atrocity and occurs alongside other atrocities; war provides the opportunity for widespread rape and many if not all male soldiers will take advantage of it.

Yet many armed groups, including some state militaries, leftist insurgent groups, and secessionist ethnic groups, do not engage in widespread rape despite frequent interaction with civilians on otherwise intimate terms. Indeed, some armed groups engage in ethnic cleansing—the classic setting for widespread rape—without engaging in sexual violence. And rape occurs in sharply varying proportions to other forms of violence in armed groups' repertoires of violence against civilians; in some cases the ratio is relatively high, in others very low.

The neglected fact of variation, including the relative absence of wartime sexual violence by one or more armed groups, has important policy implications: rape is not inevitable in war as is sometimes claimed. The neglected fact begs the questions: Under what conditions do armed groups not engage in sexual violence? Under what conditions do they engage in rape as a strategy of war?

In the past decade, a wide range of governmental, international, and nongovernmental organizations have called for policies to effectively limit wartime sexual violence, a pattern of violence that affects the most vulnerable populations in many conflict zones. I argue that analysis of variation in the pattern of such violence—in its frequency, targeting, and form—should help leaders and policymakers in developing more effective policies. That some groups do not engage in sexual violence reinforces arguments that commanders of armed groups that do engage in it as well as perpetrators should be held accountable for rape. Analyzing the internal dynamics of armed groups that do not engage in wartime sexual violence may help policymakers define effective points of intervention.

I first introduce key concepts and a typology of violence against civilians that distinguishes three dimensions of violence: targeting, whether individual, collective, or indiscriminate; strategic or opportunistic; and frequency. I then show that the dominant approaches in the literature do not account for the observed variation in wartime sexual violence against civilians. I argue that the way forward requires that researchers focus on the internal dynamics of armed groups. I then advance a way of analyzing those dynamics in order to explain variation, and show how it captures distinct logics behind both the practice of rape as a weapon of war and its absence. I conclude with suggestions about how these logics may have relevant policy implications for the curtailing of wartime sexual violence.

Key Concepts

By *absence of sexual violence*, I mean the (relative) absence of sexual violence: sexual violence by a group is very rare (but not completely absent). Throughout, *armed group* refers to both state and nonstate groups.

An *asymmetric conflict* is one in which one armed group engages in significant sexual violence against the members or supporters of another, but the latter does not respond in kind. In El Salvador, during the first years of the civil war, state forces engaged in rape against civilians in the context of massacres; yet insurgents did not rape (Wood 2003). In Vietnam, U.S. soldiers engaged in rape and sexual torture of civilians (for example, Charlie Company raped approximately 20 girls and women during the My Lai massacre); while the frequency with which it occurred is not well documented, it appears to be significantly greater than that by the North Vietnamese military and its allies (Olson and Roberts 1998; Weaver 2006).

By *repertoire of violence*: I mean the subset of battle deaths, assassination, forced displacement, torture, sexual violence (various forms), et cetera, regularly observed on the part of an armed group (Hoover 2010). Repertoires vary across armed groups: for example, rape comprises a significant fraction of violence by Bosnian Serb militias during the Balkans conflict while rape does not appear to be part of the Tamil Tigers' (LTTE) repertoire (Wood 2009). Repertoires often change significantly over time; for example, the Salvadoran military's repertoire went from being very wide, incorporating nearly all types of violence, to one less wide (though still significantly wider than that of the insurgents). A group may add a particular form of violence to its repertoire in response to another group's engaging in that form; that is, it may "mirror" the other's repertoire, either as a strategic decision by the leadership or by individual units choosing to wield violence similar in form to that observed. Or should civilians resist a group's rule, an armed group may turn more punitive on command or as a result of combatant frustration. The officially endorsed repertoire may be distinct from that observed in practice on the ground, as shown in the case of the Israeli Defense Forces during the first intifada (Ron 2000).

In accordance with recent international law, by *rape* I mean the penetration of the anus or vagina with any object or body part or of any body part of the victim or perpetrator's body with a sexual organ, by force or by threat of force or coercion, or by taking advantage of a coercive environment, or against a person incapable of giving genuine consent.[2] Thus rape can occur against men as well as women. *Sexual violence* is a broader category that includes rape, nonpenetrating sexual assault, mutilation, sexual slavery, enforced prostitution, enforced sterilization, and forced pregnancy.[3]

I make three distinctions concerning violence: targeting, purpose, and frequency, as summarized in figure 1. (Note that the typology applies to any form of violence, not just sexual violence, and also can be extended to

---

2. See Preparatory Commission for the International Criminal Court, *Elements of Crimes* (UN Doc. PNICC/2000/1/Add.2, 2000) and its reference to article 8(2) (e) (vi) 1 ICC St.

3. Ibid.

Figure 1. Typology of Violence against Civilians

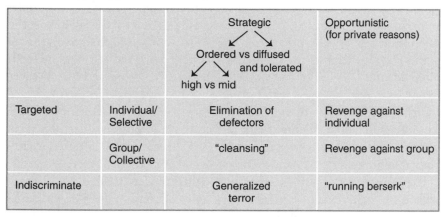

		Strategic	Opportunistic (for private reasons)
		Ordered vs diffused and tolerated high vs mid	
Targeted	Individual/ Selective	Elimination of defectors	Revenge against individual
	Group/ Collective	"cleansing"	Revenge against group
Indiscriminate		Generalized terror	"running berserk"

Third dimension: Frequency

violence against fellow members of the armed group or prisoners of war). The first set of concepts concern whom the group targets with violence. *Selective violence* is violence targeted by an armed group at an individual because of her behavior, often providing support for a rival group or some other refusal to comply (Kalyvas 2006). In contrast, *indiscriminate violence* is violence that is not targeted (indeed, in its proper form it is random). In between is *collective targeting*, the targeting by an armed group of social groups because of their identity as members of that group; examples include ethnic groups, political parties, particular villages or regions thought to support the rival, and so on.

The second distinction involves the purpose of the violence, whether it is *strategic*, that is, carried out on behalf of the group, or *opportunistic*, carried out for private (not group) reasons. Within the strategic category, a further distinction is between that which is ordered by the command structure (and whether by high-level or mid-level commanders) and that which is not ordered but is diffused across units and tolerated by the command structure, that is, what Osiel terms "atrocity by connivance" (1999, 187–93).

Finally, the third distinction concerns the level of violence: does the particular type of violence (ethnic cleansing, for example) occur very frequently, moderately often, or merely occasionally? This of course begs the question: relevant to what? At a minimum, the comparison is to other units or armed groups in the same conflict, but may include explicit cross-conflict comparison. Two further distinctions are often crucial for conceptualizing this dimension. We may be interested in the frequency of this form of violence against combatants (members of the group itself or prisoners of war) as well as against civilians (the focus of this chapter). And the measure of frequency will vary depending on the focus: the absolute number of events, the number of events per victim population (*incidence*, but note "victim population" begs precision—is it the population of some geographical area, a targeted ethnic group, the national population?) or the fraction of the victim population that suffered one or more event of this type (*prevalence*). (There is a distinct notion of frequency, which is the frequency of events compared to the number of members of the armed group: 100 incidents of rape, for example, indicate a different level of sexual violence by armed group members if they number 1,000,000 than if they number only 100 [Wood 2010].)

Before proceeding, it is important to address a doubt often raised about the claim that sexual violence on the part of some groups is very rare. Given the inadequacy of data on sexual violence, the observed absence might reflect our ignorance of its actual occurrence rather than its rarity (a negative fact very difficult to prove). Indeed, there are many reasons that rape and other forms of sexual violence are underreported in wartime (Wood 2006). The frequency and type of incidents reported are shaped by oft-noted factors such as the willingness of victims to report the crime, whether forensic authorities record signs of sexual violence, and the resources available to organizations reporting human rights abuses. Further, the description of sexual violence as "widespread" and "systematic" may reflect an organization's attempt to draw resources to document sexual violence (whatever its actual level) rather than the pattern of incidents per se. And in settings where political violence is ongoing, organizations may feel it prudent to state that all sides engage in sexual violence, whatever their beliefs and data about asymmetric patterns. Nor is it reasonable to assume that it is underreported to the same degree across conflicts, parties, and regions, as there are often regional, class, and partisan bias in the reporting rate. Reporting rates may also vary across forms of sexual violence: Rape, particularly rape of males, is likely less reported than other forms in most settings. Even when reporting occurs, available data may not identify perpetrators by unit of the armed group, but only by the armed group's name. The "gold standard" method for statistical analysis of human rights violations, multiple systems estimation, depends on the availability of at least three lists with identified victims of sufficiently dense data on violence events, a criterion which appears to be met in the case of El Salvador and perhaps one other case (Hoover 2010).

Nonetheless, the variation in the incidence and form of sexual violence is sufficiently large that it exceeds the measurement error in the reporting of the better-documented cases: the existence of very well-documented, low-incidence cases strongly suggests that not all cases of armed groups that engage in infrequent sexual violence are artifacts of ignorance. For example, it is unlikely that the apparent absence of sexual violence in the Israeli/Palestinian conflict is due to underreporting, given the scrutiny of violence there by domestic human rights groups and international actors. In short, it is unlikely, for example, that the level of rape of women and girls was so much less in Bosnia-Herzegovina or that it was so much more in Israel/Palestine as to confound the observation of significant variation.

Incomplete Explanations

What might account for the observed variation in wartime sexual violence? Various potential explanations occur in the literature, at times implicitly. I argue they are at best incomplete.

Type of Conflict

The type of conflict does not well predict this variation: both high and low prevalence of sexual violence is observed across categories. For example, sexual violence was very prevalent during and after the sieges of Nanjing and Berlin in World War II, as well as in civil conflicts such as Bosnia and Rwanda. Nor does the conflict being an ethnic, religious, or secessionist one predict high levels of sexual violence, according to the preliminary analysis of cross-national patterns by Dara Cohen (2009a). Nor is world region associated with high levels of wartime sexual violence (controlling for the number of conflicts): as a percentage of conflicts observed, those with high levels of sexual violence are no more frequent in Africa than in Eastern Europe and Asia (Cohen 2009a). Such social structural arguments are too broad to be useful.

Opportunity

One hypothesis, often implicit, is that the oft-observed increase in sexual violence during war reflects increased opportunity. Institutions of social control are often weaker in war, particularly when young combatants fight far from their home, communities are scattered to distinct areas, norms of respect for elders are undermined by new sources of authority such as guns, and armed groups loot kitchens for supplies. This approach implies that the pattern of sexual violence should mirror those of other forms of violence (because opportunity to loot and rape is also opportunity to kill) and that combatants should not target civilians of a particular ethnicity (unless opportunity depends directly on ethnicity). It also suggests that sexual violence should be higher on the part of groups that loot provisions, and more generally, that it should increase and decrease with other forms of violence.

In short, if opportunity explains sexual violence, repertoires should not vary with the targeted group (because opportunity for sexual violence is also opportunity for other violence), and sexual violence should comprise a higher fraction of the repertoire of those groups with frequent access to civilians.

Some studies weakly confirm these implications (Mitchell and Gluch 2004; Morris 1996). But in general, variation in opportunity does not account for the observed variation in sexual violence. Many armed actors target particular groups in patterns not explained by opportunity; in both Bosnia-Herzegovina and Rwanda, perpetrators had roughly equal access to civilians of various ethnicities yet targeted particular ones. The Salvadoran insurgency depended closely on residents of contested areas for supplies engaged in little sexual violence throughout the conflict.

And sexual violence does not always vary with other forms of violence. Some insurgent groups such as the LTTE in Sri Lanka and many Marxist-Leninist insurgent groups engage in significant levels of other forms of violence against civilians but rarely engage in sexual violence. Levels do not vary consistently across the repertoire of armed groups: some exert unusually high levels of sexual violence compared to other forms of violence (the Bosnian Serbs, for example), others unusually low levels (the LTTE). Although lethal violence by Salvadoran security forces decreased rapidly after 1983 as a result of pressure from the U.S. Congress, sexual torture of political prisoners continued throughout the war. Thus we should not assume that sexual violence always varies with the general level of abuse.

An obvious explanation for the absence of sexual violence against civilians is the absence of civilians, perhaps because the armed group operates far from civilian areas. However, this circumstance is likely to be rare for several reasons. First, insurgent groups nearly always depend on civilians for supplies and intelligence, and sometimes for cover as well. While state militaries may defend boundaries far from civilian areas, they nearly always also occupy cities and major towns, giving ample access to civilians for at least part of the force. Second, it is often the case that the women and children are among the last residents to flee contested zones as men, targeted more frequently with lethal violence, leave the area or join an armed group. Thus the presence of girls and women, the usual targets of rape, tends to persist, particularly on the part of poor rural populations dependent on access to land, the frequent setting of contemporary civil wars. Finally, some armed groups capture and abduct girls and women to serve as forced labor and sex slaves, sometimes holding them for long periods of time. Thus a local absence of civilians does not per se account for an absence of sexual violence.

Incentives

A distinct approach argues that wartime experience increases individual incentives to engage in sexual violence. There are several versions of this argument. Some scholars interpret wartime increases in sexual violence to the breakdown of patriarchal institutions during war (Brownmiller 1975; Enloe 1983). Arguments based on patriarchal social relations imply that sexual violence should be more prevalent in wars in which traditional gender norms are more disrupted. But in many civil wars, gender roles become *less* polarized because village hierarchies break down as the population disperses and women take on tasks normally carried out by men. It does not appear to be the case that sexual violence is higher when traditional norms are more disrupted. Contrary to the patriarchal thesis, in some conflicts patriarchal relations are so disrupted that there are significant numbers of female combatants in insurgent factions. Rather than the predicted high rates of sexual violence, rates appear to have been very low in many such groups: among them the insurgencies in Sri Lanka and El Salvador. And women sometimes participate in sexual violence as in Rwanda, where women sometimes incited men to rape, in Sierra Leone (as we will see below), and in the sexual humiliation of men detained by U.S. forces in Iraq, Guantánamo, and Afghanistan.

A second argument that does account for such targeting is that of revenge: combatants target enemy civilians with violence in revenge for the violence suffered by their community. However, why revenge takes the form of sexual rather than other kinds of violence is usually not explained. Sexual violence is sometimes said to occur in retaliation for sexual violence previously suffered (or rumored to suffer) by co-ethnics, but in asymmetric conflicts, at least one armed group does not respond in kind to sexual violence.

The militarized masculinity approach does account for the targeting of enemy women and men, and with specifically sexual violence (Morris 1996; Goldstein 2001). In order to persuade men to fight and endure the hardships of war, societies develop members willing to stand fast under fire, usually via the development of sharp distinctions between genders: to become men, boys must become warriors. Leaders persuade soldiers that to be a real man is to assert a militaristic masculinity, with the result that soldiers represent domination of the enemy in highly gendered terms and use specifically sexual violence against enemy populations. Moreover, bonding among members of the small unit—the loyalty that enables warriors to fight under the terrifying conditions of war—also takes gendered forms, reinforcing the militaristic masculinity of training.

Wartime memoirs from some conflicts (for example, memoirs by U.S. soldiers who served in Vietnam) offer anecdotal support for this approach.

Particular types of small unit bonding such as joint visits to brothels may play a role in the frequent occurrence of gang rapes in wartime. However, if this approach is to explain variation in wartime sexual violence, armies should promote different notions of masculinity, with armies that emphasize more militaristic notions of manhood responsible for higher levels of sexual violence. However, many insurgent and state armies are very effective, all-male fighting forces yet do not engage in mass rape, an indication that not all militarized forms of masculinity lead to sexual violence. Moreover, the militaristic masculinity approach does not specify well what mechanism underlies its link to sexual violence, whether armies inculcate new norms, provide incentives to reward compliance without internalization, or recruit only those attracted to militaristic practices.

Rape as a Substitution for Consensual Sex

According to the substitution argument, if combatants do not have regular access to prostitutes, camp followers, or willing civilians, they will turn to rape. As Cynthia Enloe (2000) points out, some military officials appear to assume that "recreational rape" occurs when soldiers are not adequately supplied with sexual partners. One reason for the rapid expansion of military brothels (the so-called "comfort women" system) by Japanese military authorities after the widespread rape of civilians in Nanjing was to avoid such incidents in the future. At a recent conference I attended, a military official argued that the reason for the prevalence of rape in the eastern DRC was that combatants were too poor to pay prostitutes.

However, the substitution argument does not explain the frequently observed targeting of particular groups of women, nor the often extreme violence that frequently accompanies wartime rape, nor the occurrence of sexual torture. And if this argument were complete, we would not see rape by forces with ample access to prostitutes. This is certainly not always the case, as evident in the rape of girls and women by members of the U.S. military in Vietnam. Similarly, combatants of the Revolutionary United Front (RUF) of Sierra Leone engaged in frequent rape of civilians despite their access to girls and women held as sex slaves. The argument rests on a number of unexamined assumptions: that only sexual relations with females gratify sexual desire, that sexual desire is so strong as to override countervailing factors, that rape in fact satisfies sexual and not some other type of desire, and that sufficiently many men act on these assumptions to explain widespread rape as occurring because of the absence of prostitutes or consensual sexual partners.

Female Combatants

Finally, an explanation sometimes made for the absence of sexual violence on the part of some armed groups is the presence of many female cadre. However, the causal mechanism is not well specified; candidates include the following. One is the substitution argument: the presence of female combatants means that male combatants do not "need" to rape. But some armed groups with significant numbers of female combatants do engage in high levels of sexual violence; the RUF of Sierra Leone is an example. Moreover, female combatants themselves actively engage in it in some conflicts: according to Dara Cohen (2009c), female combatants participated in 25 percent of the RUF's gang rapes (which comprise about 75 percent of the total). Or perhaps the presence of women disrupts male bonding through misogynist training practices that inculcate militaristic masculinity. However, the experience of female soldiers in U.S. forces is that such practices continue in more muted and covert form, despite their official banning (Hillman 2009). An organization might prohibit sexual violence by its cadre for fear that the enemy would retaliate in kind, threatening its own female cadre. Or an organization may pursue a strategy or ideology (for example, recruitment based on sexual violence by enemy forces) that both appeals to female recruits and also promotes the prohibition of sexual violence.

Sexual Violence as Instrumental for the Group

In the explanations based on increased opportunity and incentive, sexual violence occurred for reasons of individual gratification or as a by-product of supposedly necessary training. In contrast, some armed groups promote (or tolerate) sexual violence as an effective means toward group goals. While strategic sexual violence may not be explicitly ordered, it is (at least) tolerated; if any punishment occurs it is symbolic and limited, clearly for external consumption rather than deterrence. Such violence appears to take two broad forms. The first is sexual torture, sexual slavery, or sexual humiliation of persons detained by an armed group (custodial sexual violence). The second is widespread sexual violence as a form of terror or collective punishment targeted at a particular group, which frequently takes the form of gang (and often public) rape, usually over an extended period of time, most notoriously as part of some campaigns of "ethnic cleansing," to force the movement of entire populations from particular regions claimed as the homeland, and as part of some genocides. In addition, commanders may see violence, including sexual violence, as a low-cost reward to troops, "Count Tilly's reward" (Mitchell 2004).

International criminal courts have ruled that sexual violence was systematic with evidence of command responsibility in two cases, ruling rape a crime against humanity in Bosnia and a form of genocide in Rwanda. Other cases include Guatemala, where rape by state forces was widespread in the context of sweeps through indigenous villages in the highlands, and Peru, where custodial rape occurred in military bases and prisons, sites under direct command control (Leiby 2009). The Truth Commission in Guatemala found direct evidence of commander promotion of rape of civilians in the form of ridicule of combatants who initially declined to participate (cited in Leiby 2009).

However, this argument predicts more sexual violence than is observed: if sexual violence is so effective a strategy of war, why don't all armed groups engage in it? The conditions for such instrumental promotion of sexual violence are not well identified in the literature. Some authors suggest that patriarchal culture provides the relevant condition: where armed groups understand sexual violence as a violation of the family's and community's honor, they are likely to engage in sexual violence as a weapon of war (Enloe 2000). However, this appears to predict significantly more sexual violence than is in fact observed, as such beliefs are present in many societies where massive sexual violence on the scale implicitly predicted by this argument has not occurred, as in Sri Lanka, El Salvador, and Israel/Palestine. Moreover, such broad notions of cultural proclivity do not account for cases where one party to the war promotes sexual violence while the other does not. Nor does the literature adequately explore whether sexual violence is a strategic choice by group leadership (either at the apex or at some other point in the chain of command) that is effectively enforced by the group hierarchy. If so, sexual violence should vary with command-and-control cohesion, discipline within armed faction. Or is it a practice diffused across small units (perhaps from other armies) and tolerated by the military hierarchy? I return to this issue below.

In sum, the literature at best explains only part of the observed variation as it generally overpredicts wartime sexual violence and fails to explain the fact that many armed groups do not engage in high or even moderate levels of sexual violence. Moreover, it usually assumes rather than explains why violence (sometimes) takes sexual form. The scope conditions for arguments are generally underspecified.

Theoretical Framework

That these diverse arguments do not explain the observed variation suggests that research should focus on variation in the dynamics internal to armed groups. In what follows, I develop a theoretical framework to fully account for variation that emphasizes the norms of combatants, leaders' strategic choices of repertoire and institutions for training and discipline, and the dynamics within small units once deployed in war. I assume that armed groups are complex organizations that attempt to control and direct violence by their members, if only to the minimal extent that combatants should not turn their arms on their commanders. I discuss each element of the framework drawing on and adapting the sociological literature on state militaries and extending it to insurgent groups.

Individual Combatants

Armed groups draw their members from particular cultural settings, usually a particular patriarchy. Incoming recruits carry with them cultural norms and beliefs concerning the appropriateness of different kinds of violence, including sexual violence, against particular populations. Armed groups may draw from particular subgroups, for example a specific ethnic group, precisely for these reasons. Some groups, for example some paramilitary groups, actively attempt to recruit from criminal populations. State militaries often attempt to draw or conscript recruits from a wide range of subcultures in order to build national unity. The relevant pool of recruits may also reflect the organization's resource base: Those without economic resources are more likely to attract "activist" recruits willing to make long-term commitments to ideological goals (Weinstein 2007). Whether or not recruits enter an armed organization with relatively homogeneous norms and beliefs thus depends on the recruiting practices of the organization. Those norms and beliefs may be profoundly altered as recruits are inducted into the group through both formal and informal practices, as discussed below.

Leadership Strategy

Military leaders seek to control the repertoire, targeting, and frequency of violence wielded by their combatants, not least because of the fear that weapons wielded by soldiers may be turned against officers (Huntington 1957). Likely considerations include not only issues of military tactics and strategy but also implications for the ongoing supply of recruits, intelligence, other necessary "inputs" to the war effort, and for the legitimacy of the war effort in the eyes of desired supporters (domestic and international alike). Even when an armed group appears to embrace terrorizing of civilians, there are decisions to be made about targeting and timing. In particular, military leaders may make explicit decisions to prohibit or to promote sexual violence (of different forms, against particular groups). If it occurs at a significant level, leaders who have not yet made an explicit decision may be pressed to do so and may decide to tolerate its occurrence without an explicit decision to prohibit or promote. And of course commanders may

promote high levels of violence toward civilians without a formal decision to do so using euphemisms understood as signaling to combatants
that they will not be punished. Or leaders may delegate certain forms of
violence to groups they claim not to command, for example, militias or
death squads.

In order to control violence, group leaders (or their delegates) also develop institutions for the socialization and training of recruits and for the
discipline of members. To highly varying degrees, those institutions may
also attempt to distill group ideology (Hoover 2010).

Institutions for Combatant Socialization

To build an effective armed group, recruits have to be melded into effective combatants through training and socialization. Since Stouffer et al.'s
analysis of tens of thousands of interviews with U.S. soldiers during World
War II, most military leaders have understood that men hold fast under
fire not because of grand concepts such as patriotism or group ideology
but because of their commitments to their "primary group" of fellow combatants (Shils and Janowitz 1948). For example, the sustained fighting
ability of the Wehrmacht until nearly the end of World War II was at-
tributed to such "primary group" cohesion (Shils and Janowitz 1948; Bartov 1991). One reason given for poor morale among U.S. soldiers late in
the war in Vietnam was low group cohesion resulting from patterns of
individual rather than group rotation into and out of the war theater.

For an effective army, not only do recruits have to stand fast under fire,
they also need to fire their weapons. According to S. L. A. Marshall (summarized in Grossman 1996), in World War II, only about 15 percent of
U.S. troops in combat fired; in the Korean War about 50 percent did; in
Vietnam about 95 percent did so. Dave Grossman (and others) attributes
the dramatic increase in firing rates to increasingly realistic training that
conditions recruits to battlefield conditions. However, recent work has
thrown doubt on the claims about low World War II firing rates (Spiller
1988; Smoler 1989). In any case, strong identification with the primary
group as well as military training contributes to firing rates, as it absolves
the combatant of individual responsibility for the wielding of violence.

Training and socialization to the small group takes place both formally
through group institutions such as boot camp and informally through initiation rituals and hazing. In state militaries, the powerful experiences of
endless drilling, dehumanization through abuse at the hands of the drill
sergeant, and degradation and then "rebirth" as group members through
initiation rituals typically meld recruits into combatants whose loyalties
are often felt to be stronger than those to family (Winslow 1999; Nuwer
2004).

The result is a setting where conformity effects are likely to be extremely strong. Armed groups manage member emotions through highly standardized, repetitive, collective rituals, as in the expression of grief through a single volley fire at military funerals (Jelusic 2005). Brutalization of recruits is intended to enhance aggression, which the discipline of drill is intended to control (Grossman 1996; Osiel 1999). In some state militaries, training and hazing rely on abusive gendered stereotypes to reshape individual identities and to build group cohesion, evident (until recently) in the rhetoric of U.S. drill sergeants—recruits are "ladies" and "fags"—and the misogyny of marching chants—"This is my rifle; this is my gun [hand on crotch], This is for fighting; this is for fun" (Burke 2004; Goldstein 2001).

Insurgent groups socialize recruits in a variety of ways. Jeremy Weinstein (2007) argues that, in contrast to groups with economic endowments that draw opportunistic recruits and tend to wield violence indiscriminately, groups with social endowments draw activist recruits willing to make commitments to group goals over long time horizons. Such groups insist on extensive indoctrination and training. However, in his emphasis on contrasting pools of recruits, Weinstein underestimates the power of socialization practices and disciplinary institutions to meld recruits—typically male teenagers—into group members irrespective of their initial motives for joining. That is, the distinct patterns of violence may reflect group strategy concerning training, discipline, and incentives and group ideology rather than distinct pools of recruits (Wood 2009; Hoover 2010). For example, Francisco Gutiérrez Sanín (2008) shows in his comparison of paramilitary and guerrilla combatants in Colombia that initial socialization, discipline, and incentives are sufficiently different as to account for differences in violence between the two groups. To the extent that the organization relies on child recruits, training and socialization are particularly more likely to play a more important role than time horizons.

Armed group institutions attempt to inculcate group ideology in highly varying degrees. Some armed groups, often leftist groups that understand their armed struggle as likely to continue over many years and perhaps decades, go to impressive lengths to inculcate group ideology and identification long after the initial training period. In her research analyzing the contrasting repertoires of violence on the part of state and insurgent forces during El Salvador's civil war (and contrasting repertoires on the part of subgroups within each side), Amelia Hoover (2010) finds that armed groups that employ both strong disciplinary systems and consistent political education regimes (in this case the insurgents, particularly the faction Fuerzas Populares de Liberación) use narrower repertoires of violence and in particular do not engage in sexual violence.

Wartime Dynamics

Combatant norms and practices—both general cultural ones and also those instilled during training—may evolve dramatically during active engagement. Both the suffering and wielding of violence may bring profound changes to combatants' understanding of the appropriateness of repertoires, targeting, and frequency of violence. The increasing desensitization of combatants to violence and the dehumanizing of victims, the anxiety and uncertainty of combat and the threat of violence, the displacement of responsibility not only onto the group but onto the enemy who "deserves what they got" (blame attribution) are powerful wartime processes that may reshape group repertoires toward the wider use of violence, wider both in the sense of wider targeted and broader repertoire (Browning 1992; Hoover 2010; Hinton 2005; Chirot and McCauley 2006). Collective responsibility for atrocities can itself become a source of group cohesion and a bulwark against betrayal (Osiel 1999; Goldstein 2001). Indeed, small group dynamics can undermine military discipline when small group loyalties and conformity effects within the group lead to withholding of information from commanding officers, disobedience, or the extreme example of the "fragging" of U.S. officers in Vietnam (MacCoun 1993; Bourke 1999).

Military Hierarchy

The strength of the military hierarchy determines whether the leadership's choices about violence or those of combatants shape the observed repertoire, targeting, and frequency of violence by the armed group. Given the challenges of organizing and controlling violence toward group goals, armed groups tend to be hierarchical (Huntington 1957; Siebold 2001). Whether decisions of the leadership are effectively enforced down the chain of command within the armed group depends on the strength of the military hierarchy. Within an armed organization—particularly in the changing and often covert circumstances of irregular warfare—there are a series of principal-agent relationships down the chain of command in which the superior officer as the principal attempts to influence the behavior of those below (his or her agents, who have distinct interests from those of the principal) but without access to the same information (Gates 2002; Mitchell 2004; Butler, Gluch, and Mitchell 2007). The ability of the hierarchy to enforce decisions concerning patterns of violence thus depends on the flow of information concerning those patterns up the chain of command and the willingness of superiors to hold those below them accountable, typically through both punishment and positive rewards.

High levels of "secondary group cohesion" on the part of combatants, that is, strong identification with military units above the most immediate and with the armed group as a whole, are one way to the resolution of principal-agent tensions and thus for a strong military hierarchy (Siebold 2001). When military superiors are seen as legitimate authorities, the likelihood of obedience even in the wielding of extreme violence is greatly enhanced (Milgram 1974; Grossman 1996).

This challenge of resolving principal-agent problems applies to insurgent groups as well: leaders attempt to control the violence of their combatants; whether they succeed in doing so depends on the strength of the hierarchy linking combatants and leaders. For example, Humphreys and Weinstein (2006) found that unit cohesion and discipline, rather than the level of contestation, social structure such as community or ethnic ties, or the existence of a local economic surplus, best explained patterns of civilian abuse across armed groups in Sierra Leone.

However, the irregular warfare strategy adopted by many nonstate armed groups enormously complicates the ability of the hierarchy to enforce decisions. Units may operate independently for significant periods of time with little direct contact with superiors in the hierarchy with the result that little information about unit practices flows up the hierarchy and superiors have little opportunity to punish infractions by subordinates. Insurgent groups manage the challenge of sustaining a command and control hierarchy in different ways and to different degrees. To minimize damage from interrogation of captured cadre, members may in fact know little about the group beyond the small unit. Unless the insurgent group controls a significant area, training of new recruits is covert and may be interrupted. For example, the North Vietnamese Army model of three-person small units headed by a party cadre combined strong primary group cohesion with ongoing surveillance of the primary group by the party, a combination argued to account for the army's resilience in the face of U.S. firepower (Henderson 1979).

When Is Wartime Rape a Strategy of War?

The theoretical framework is of course relevant for analysis of all forms of violence, not just sexual violence. In what follows, I focus on the implications that are particularly relevant for analysis of patterns of sexual violence, particularly that of rape as a strategy of war and the absence of sexual violence on the part of some armed groups. For both, I identify two logics, a top-down and a bottom-across logic.

Before doing so, however, what happens when the orders of superiors and the intentions of combatants about sexual violence collide? If the military hierarchy is sufficiently strong, the choice of the leadership will prevail, whether it is promotion, prohibition, or tolerance. For example, if leaders judge sexual violence to be counterproductive to their interests and if the hierarchy is sufficiently strong, little sexual violence will be observed. In the contrasting case, an organization with an effective hierarchy could judge sexual violence as in its interest and effectively enforce such violence by its combatants. If hierarchical strength is insufficient, individual and unit norms will dominate, with the organization unable to deter or promote behavior it would rather prevent. Thus under some, probably rare conditions, the prevalence of sexual violence may be low without relying on hierarchical discipline, namely when sufficiently many combatants have themselves internalized norms against sexual violence (see below). More frequent is the other case of an organization's prohibiting sexual violence but without the hierarchy or will to effectively do so.

The strength of the hierarchy (the ability of the hierarchy to enforce decisions taken by the leadership) is thus central to the theoretical framework and its implications. For the framework to be useful in analyzing repertoires of violence, the degree of hierarchical strength must be observable apart from patterns of violence, in particular sexual violence, against civilians. Observable indicators of organizational strength include the ability to effectively tax the civilian population and to channel the resulting resources throughout the organization with low levels of corruption, the organization's routine punishment of combatants who break rules and norms other than those concerning violence toward civilians (a sufficient but not a necessary condition for a strong hierarchy, as the hierarchy may be so strong that combatants never break the rules), and the organization's capacity to carry out widespread and/or complex offensive or defensive maneuvers that require extensive coordination of multiple units.

Explaining the Absence of Sexual Violence: Two Logics

THE TOP-DOWN LOGIC

What considerations would lead commanders and leaders to attempt to effectively prohibit sexual violence by combatants? An armed group's leadership may prohibit sexual violence for strategic, normative, or practical reasons (Wood 2009). First, many armed groups fear the consequences of uncontrolled violence by their combatants: such forces may be unready to counter a surprise attack, they may prove difficult to bring back under control, and they may even turn their sights on their commanders. And unintended consequences may be severe, such as the entry of an ally of the enemy into the fray. If an organization aspires to govern the civilian

population, leaders will probably attempt to restrain combatants' engagement in sexual violence against those civilians (though perhaps endorsing
it against other civilian groups) for fear of undermining support for their
present armed struggle and their future rule. Similarly, if an armed group
is dependent on civilians for supplies or for high-quality intelligence—
which is difficult to coerce (Wood 2003)—leaders will probably attempt to
restrain sexual violence against those civilians. The Sri Lankan insurgency
killed thousands of civilians in the course of assassinations by suicide bombing and collective reprisals yet did not engage in sexual violence toward civilians despite its practice of ethnic cleansing, a pattern best explained by
the top-down logic of the absence of sexual violence given the group's demonstrated ability to effectively collect taxes and punish combatants for infractions of its code of conduct (Wood 2009).

Reasons for prohibiting sexual violence may reflect normative concerns
as well as practical constraints. Members of a revolutionary group seeking
to carry out a social revolution may see themselves as the disciplined bearers
of a new, more just social order for all citizens and therefore prohibit sexual violence because such violence violates the norms of the new society or
as a means of legitimizing that ideology both to members and to its likely
constituents. Nationalist and anticolonial insurgencies may prohibit sexual violence and seek female cadre as part of its ideological commitment
to becoming a modern state army. Leninist groups may suppress sexual
violence as part of the general emphasis on discipline and self-sacrifice,
and its commitment (in varying degrees) to gender equality. Relatedly, in
conflicts where one party engages in massive violence against civilians,
the other party may not do so as an explicit strategy to demonstrate moral
superiority. A norm against sexual violence may take a distinct form: sexual
violence across ethnic boundaries may be understood by leaders or combatants as polluting the instigator rather than harming and humiliating
the targeted individual and community.

New social norms against the use of particular forms of violence and in
favor of others may also be actively cultivated by an armed group as a matter of strategy or principle. The Salvadoran insurgency attempted to shape
individual longings for revenge toward a more general aspiration for justice because revenge seeking by individuals would undermine insurgent
discipline and obedience (Wood 2003). Despite systematic celebration of
martyrdom in pursuit of victory, the insurgency did not endorse suicide
missions and effectively prohibited sexual violence.

Finally, leaders may prohibit sexual violence out of deference to international law for various reasons, perhaps because they aspire to some sort
of international recognition or because they fear financial backers may
disapprove.

Armed groups that rely on female combatants may have additional reasons to restrain sexual violence on the part of their troops. If female combatants are valued, commanders may fear that sexual violence against civilians may evolve into sexual violence against fellow group members, undermining group cohesion and morale. Or commanders may fear that sexual violence by combatants may deter future female recruits, for fear of suffering or witnessing such violence, if female combatants do not in fact welcome sexual violence against enemies. (Of course an armed group may attract female recruits and effectively prohibit sexual violence for a third, unrelated reason such as those given in the previous paragraph.) Commanders may fear that their own civilians or combatants may be targeted with sexual violence in revenge should their own combatants engage in it.

The Bottom-Across Logic

If commanders prohibit sexual violence or promote it but the hierarchy is too weak to enforce that policy, whether or not combatants engage in sexual violence depends on individual and small unit norms. If individual combatants and their units endorse and enforce norms against sexual violence, little sexual violence by those combatants will occur. Such norms may take the form of internalized cultural norms or group codes of conduct whereby noncombatants are viewed as beyond the circle of legitimate violence. In particular, sexual relations with civilians associated with the enemy may be understood as polluting to the perpetrator, or for other reasons be normatively prohibited. Or they may be norms comprising an internalized self-perception on the part of members as a liberating rather than an occupying or punishing force. (Note that the norms themselves may originate with the leadership; the issue is whether they have been internalized as norms by individual combatants.) A practice of not engaging in rape could spread across units (just as the practice of rape could spread) as the correct interpretation of traditional norms in the setting of war.

The conditions for such shunning of sexual violence by combatants are demanding (Hoover 2007). The wartime processes of brutalization, desensitization, and dehumanization discussed above must not have eroded such normative constraints. And given the powerful influence of small group dynamics in armed units, all or nearly all combatants must endorse the norm, and enforce it against the few who attempt to transgress it. The chances of a practice of not engaging in rape diffusing across units are likely higher if the armed group itself endorses and attempts to reinforce such norms.

Explaining Rape as a Strategy (or Tactic) of War: Two Logics

Top-Down Logic: Rape as a Strategy of War

As we saw above, sexual violence may be promoted by group leadership as a strategy of war as part of the group's repertoire of violence against particular populations as in the case of sexual torture of political prisoners or against members of particular groups as they are "cleansed" from an area, as an appropriate form of collective punishment (as when Stalin responded to reports of rape in East Prussia with "We lecture our soldiers too much. Let them have some initiative" [Naimark 1995, 71]), or as a low-cost reward to troops.

As also noted above, the perceived effectiveness of rape raises the question of why more armed groups do not embrace it as a strategy of war ordered by commanders (rather than tolerated; see below). The conditions are the inverse of those for the absence of sexual violence: commanders must see the costs in terms of governability of troops, civilian loyalty and active cooperation (as opposed to mere compliance), and violation of domestic and international norms as outweighed by the benefits of a terrorized population, "cleansed" territory, and sated troops. Of course the common response of military and political leaders to accusation of sexual violence by troops is the claim that the troops were "out of control," an issue I return to in the conclusion.

Bottom-Across Logic: Rape as a Tactic of War

Combatants and small units may practice sexual violence that was not ordered because they perceive it as an effective tactic of war (tactic not strategy given its innovation at low levels of the command structure in this case) for reasons similar to those of commanders: as a form of effective terror, as punishment (collective or individual), or as a reward to service. If the practice spreads across units, the group's military hierarchy demonstrably tolerates its occurrence either implicitly (no explicit policy but an effective practice of toleration as there is no attempt to abrogate or punish) or explicitly with a policy of no punishment or accountability for sexual violence.

Dara Cohen (2009b) argues that gang rape was such a practice on the part of the RUF in Sierra Leone. As a result of its practice of forced recruitment (87 percent of combatants reported being forced to join), the RUF faced a particular problem of building group cohesion. Gang rape effectively built cohesion, she argues, because it was an act understood by participants to be very costly (not only breaking social norms but perhaps resulting in syphilis, which might go untreated in the context), a transformative ritual practice that broke recruits' ties to their communities and cemented new ones to the group. Indeed, as mentioned above, she finds that female combatants participated in approximately a quarter of gang rape events. In her analysis of cross-national data on wartime sexual violence, she shows that nonstate armed groups that practice forced recruitment are more likely to engage in high levels of sexual violence (Cohen 2009a).

Conclusion

Seeing sexual violence as part of a repertoire of violence and analyzing patterns of violence by a particular armed group along the distinct dimensions developed in the typology may help policymakers establish accountability for sexual violence on the part of that group. In the hope that the argument presented here may strengthen the efforts of those government, military, and insurgent leaders, UN officials, and members of nongovernmental organizations who seek to end sexual violence and other violations of the laws of war, I offer some tentative policy implications.

Building on the typology's distinction between two forms of strategic sexual violence, that between ordered violence versus violence diffused across units and tolerated by the command structure, the chapter identified two logics underlying the absence of sexual violence: the top-down logic and bottom-across logic. The bottom-across logic suggests a possible avenue of policy development: to strengthen traditional cultural and/or religious norms against sexual violence. However, once a pattern of sexual violence emerges as a practice by group members, the challenge is to interrupt peer dynamics within the armed group that reinforce the practice of sexual violence as proving virility or masculinity or as entitlement of victory. Unfortunately, in precisely such settings, armed groups tend to displace and sharply undermine the authority of traditional leaders (Wood 2008b). Lessons could perhaps be learned from campaigns against the practice of female genital cutting, the success of which often depends not on persuasion of individual family members but on widespread community pledges not to require cutting as a condition of marriageability of daughters. Ideally, reinforcing traditional norms against sexual violence would be possible without also reenforcing gender inegalitarian practices and beliefs.

The top-down logic for the absence of sexual violence suggests other avenues of policy innovation. Groups that sincerely seek to prohibit sexual violence but whose members engage in it nonetheless might seek to strengthen their institutions and hierarchy by copying the practices of ongoing political education and internal discipline of those groups that do effectively prohibit it. This may not be a practical suggestion as it implies a willingness to thoroughly revise how the group resolves principal agent problems throughout the chain of command, but should be noted nonetheless. And of course policies by international and domestic actors to promote the strengthening of military hierarchies may be controversial in many settings.

The top-down logic of strategic sexual violence might be interrupted by increasing the costs to commanders of the practice via the frequently repeated mantra of ending impunity: prosecution of commanders as well as perpetrators would increase the costs to the armed group, strengthening incentives to effectively prohibit its occurrence. Prosecution of sexual violence as a war crime, crime against humanity (as part of widespread or systematic attack on civilian population—note that sexual violence itself need not be widespread or systematic), or as genocide would increase the costs more than its prosecution under other relevant law. The same argument applies to groups where the pattern of sexual violence follows the bottom-across logic of diffusion across units with the toleration of the command structure: increasing the costs of toleration would strengthen commander incentives to punish combatants for sexual violence. In short, the implication is to strengthen commander incentives to build strong disciplinary institutions to effectively prohibit sexual violence.

Direct indicators of sexual violence as a policy include copies of orders, credible combatant reports of such orders, credible reports that combatants who refused to participate were punished, and abrogation from above of attempts to curtail the practice. Direct evidence of orders is unlikely, however; indeed, increasingly so as international prosecution of sexual violence occurs more frequently. Arguably, commands that use euphemisms for general terror such as "total war" or "all forms of vengeance" where they are unqualified by any phrase such as "against enemy troops" or where they explicitly include violence against civilians may support a claim of sexual violence as a strategy of war, as such commands establish a climate of tolerance for human rights violations, in the same way that allowing a hostile workplace climate that is permissive of harassment supports charges of sexual harassment in some countries.

This raises of course the question of how to prove command responsibility for sexual violence in the absence of direct proof. The Trial Chamber of the International Criminal Tribunal for Rwanda held that "three essential elements of command responsibility are: (1) the existence of a superior–subordinate relationship of effective control between the accused and the perpetrator of the crime; and (2) the knowledge, or constructive knowledge, of the accused that the crime was about to be, was being, or had been committed; and (3) the failure of the accused to take the necessary and reasonable measures to prevent or stop the crime, or to punish the perpetrator" (quoted in Leiby 2009, 456). The third element is relatively straightforward so I do not discuss it here.

In the absence of direct evidence that sexual violence was ordered and in the face of leaders' claims that they did not exercise effective control of troops, how might "effective control" be documented? The analysis above suggests some indicators of an effective chain of command. First, the ability of leaders to command combatants into harm's way is itself evidence of effective command: a key indicator of loss of command is the refusal of troops to engage in combat (and of course their firing weapons at commanders). Evidence of effective control is still stronger in the case that the armed group carries out offensive or defensive maneuvers over an extended area or period, as orders must be transmitted down the chain of command, and information about present position and capacity as well as intelligence about enemy position must travel up the chain of command. And it is stronger still if such movements require coordination across many different units. Second, an armed group that is able to gather and distribute financial resources across various branches of its organization without substantial "deviation" of those resources for private purposes demonstrates a cohesive command structure. Third, if an armed group routinely punishes its members for breaking rules other than those nominally prohibiting sexual violence, arguably it could also, if it chose to, punish combatants for sexual violence.

Other indirect indicators of effective control include the occurrence of sexual violence in military bases, prisons, or state-run facilities (that is, sites that are uncontroversially under commander control), against political opponents, when commanding officers are present, under order of commanding officers, or when commanding officers themselves participate in sexual violence (Leiby 2009, 438, table 3). In some contexts evidence of collective targeting of particular groups suggests purposeful engagement in sexual violence, as it suggests commanders effectively prohibit sexual violence against groups not so targeted.

Rape is not an unavoidable collateral damage of war. Its victims—women and men of all ages—were not brought down by cross fire or an errant missile. They were intentionally violated; the question then is: Is anyone beyond the immediate perpetrator responsible for the crime? Armed groups—nonstate actors as well as state militaries—often choose effectively to limit sexual violence by their members, to exclude sexual violence from their repertoire. The fact that many armed groups do not engage in sexual violence should help to put the stigma of sexual violence on the perpetrators rather than the victims of sexual violence and to strengthen accountability for sexual violence.

References

Bartov, O. 1991. *Hitler's Army*. Oxford: Oxford University Press.

Bourke, J. 1999. *An Intimate History of Killing: Face-to-Face Killing in Twentieth Century Warfare*. London: Granta Books.

Browning, C. 1992. *Ordinary Men: Reserve Police Battalion 101 and the Final Solution in Poland*. New York: HarperCollins.

Brownmiller, S. 1975. *Against Our Will: Men, Women, and Rape*. New York: Ballantine.

Burke, C. 2004. *Camp All-American, Hanoi Jane, and the High-and-Tight*. Boston: Beacon Press.

Butler, C., T. Gluch, and N. Mitchell. 2007. "Security Forces and Sexual Violence: A Cross-National Analysis of a Principal-Agent Argument." *Journal of Peace Research* 44:669–87.

Chirot, D., and C. McCauley. 2006. *Why Not Kill Them All? The Logic and Prevention of Mass Political Murder*. Princeton, NJ: Princeton University Press.

Cohen, D. 2009a. "The Causes of Sexual Violence by Insurgents during Civil War: Cross-National Evidence." Unpublished paper.

Cohen, D. 2009b. "Explaining Sexual Violence during Civil War: Evidence from Sierra Leone." Unpublished paper.

Cohen, D. 2009c. "Female Combatants and Violence in Armed Groups: Women and Wartime Rape in Sierra Leone." Unpublished paper.

Enloe, C. 1983. *Does Khaki Become You? The Militarisation of Women's Lives*. Cambridge, MA: South End Press.

Enloe, C. 2000. *Maneuvers: The International Politics of Militarizing Women's Lives*. Berkeley: University of California Press.

Gates, S. 2002. "Recruitment and Allegiance: The Microfoundations of Rebellion." *Journal of Conflict Resolution* 46:111–30.

Goldstein, J. S. 2001. *War and Gender: How Gender Shapes the War System and Vice Versa*. Cambridge: Cambridge University Press.

Grossman, D. 1996. *On Killing: The Psychological Cost of Learning to Kill in War and Society*. Boston: Little Brown.

Henderson, W. 1979. *Why the Vietcong Fought: A Study of Motivation and Control in a Modern Army in Combat*. Westport, CT: Greenwood Press.

Hillman, E. 2009. "Front and Center: Sexual Violence in U.S. Military Law." *Politics and Society* 37:101–29.

Hinton, A. 2005. *Why Did They Kill? Cambodia in the Shadow of Genocide*. Berkeley: University of California Press.

Hoover, A. 2007. "Disaggregating Violence during Armed Conflict: Why and How." Unpublished manuscript.

Hoover, A. 2010. "The 'Puzzle of Good Behavior': Background, Theory and Hypotheses." Unpublished paper.

Humphreys, M., and J. Weinstein. 2006. "Handling and Manhandling Civilians in Civil War." *American Political Science Review* 100:429–47.

Huntington, S. 1957. *The Soldier and the State. The Theory and Politics of Civil–Military Relations*. Cambridge, MA: Harvard University Press, Belknap Press.

Jelusic, L. 2005. "Ritualization of Emotions in Military Organizations." In *New Directions in Military Sociology*, ed. E. Ailed. Whitby, Ontario: de Sitter Publications.

Kalyvas, S. 2006. *The Logic of Violence in Civil War*. Cambridge: Cambridge University Press.

Leiby, M. 2009. "Wartime Sexual Violence in Guatemala and Peru." *International Studies Quarterly* 53:445–68.

MacCoun, R. 1993. "What Is Known about Unit Cohesion and Military Performance." Chapter 10 in National Defense Research Institute, *Sexual Orientation and U.S. Military Personnel Policy: Policy Options and Assessment.* Santa Monica, CA: RAND.

Milgram, S. 1974. *Obedience to Authority: An Experimental View.* New York: Harper and Row.

Mitchell, N. 2004. *Agents of Atrocity: Leaders, Followers, and the Violation of Human Rights in Civil War.* New York: Palgrave Macmillan.

Mitchell, N., and T. Gluch. 2004. "The Principals and Agents of Political Violence and the Strategic and Private Benefits of Rape." Paper presented at the annual meeting of the American Political Science Association, Chicago, September.

Morris, M. 1996. "By Force of Arms." *Duke Law Journal* 45:651–781.

Naimark, N. M. 1995. "Soviet Soldiers, German Women, and the Problem of Rape." In *The Russians in Germany: A History of the Soviet Zone of Occupation, 1945–1949.* Cambridge, MA: Harvard University Press, Belknap Press.

Nuwer, H. 2004. "Military Hazing." In *The Hazing Reader,* ed. H. Nuwer. Bloomington: Indiana University Press.

Olson, J., and R. Roberts, eds. 1998. "Summary of Rapes, 1970. Document 36." In *My Lai: A Brief History with Documents.* Boston: Bedford Books.

Osiel, M. 1999. *Obeying Orders: Atrocity, Military Discipline, and the Law of War.* New Brunswick, NJ: Transaction Publishers.

Ron, J. 2000. "Savage Restraint: Israel, Palestine and the Dialectics of Legal Repression." *Social Problems* 47:445–72.

Sanín, F. G. 2008. "Telling the Difference: Guerrillas and Paramilitaries in the Colombian War." *Politics and Society* 36:3–34.

Shils, E., and M. Janowitz. 1948. "Cohesion and Disintegration in the Wehrmacht in World War II." *Public Opinion Quarterly* 12:280–315.

Siebold, G. 2001. "Core Issues and Theory in Military Sociology." *Journal of Political and Military Sociology* 29:140–59.

Smoler, F. 1989. "The Secret of the Soldiers Who Didn't Shoot." *American Heritage Magazine* 40.2 (March). Available at www.americanheritage.com/articles/magazine/ah/1989/2/1989_2_36.shtml (accessed 10 March 2010).

Spiller, R. 1988. "S. L. A. Marshall and the Ratio of Fire." *Royal United Service Institute Journal,* Winter, 63–71.

Weaver, G. 2006. "Ideologies of Forgetting: American Erasure of Women's Sexual Trauma in the Vietnam War." PhD diss., University of Houston.

Weinstein, J. M. 2007. *Inside Rebellion: The Politics of Insurgent Violence.* Cambridge: Cambridge University Press.

Winslow, D. 1999. "Rites of Passage and Group Bonding in the Canadian Airborne." *Armed Forces and Society* 25:429–57.

Wood, E. J. 2003. *Insurgent Collective Action and Civil War in El Salvador.* Cambridge: Cambridge University Press.

Wood, E. J. 2006. "Variation in Sexual Violence during War." *Politics and Society* 34:307–41.

Wood, E. J. 2008a. "Sexual Violence during War: Toward an Understanding of Variation." In *Order, Conflict and Violence,* ed. S. Kalyvas, T. Masoud, and I. Shapiro. Cambridge: Cambridge University Press.

Wood, E. J. 2008b. "The Social Processes of Civil War: The Wartime Transformation of Social Networks." *Annual Review of Political Science* 11:539–61.

Wood, E. J. 2009. "Armed Groups and Sexual Violence: When Is Wartime Rape Rare?" *Politics and Society* 37:131–61.

Wood, E. J. 2010. "Perpetrator Propensity: Human Rights Violations per capita of the Armed Group." Unpublished paper.

4

Sexual Violence in the Post-Yugoslav Wars

Inger Skjelsbæk

R ape in war has strong historical, mythological, and cultural inter-
connections. War provides a setting in which looting and rape
act as two sides of the same coin. Rape in war is a metaphor for
war's barbarism, as well as a direct manifestation of the misuse of power
and violence unleashed by war. Rape is a metaphor for political acts. The
attack on the city of Nanjing in 1937 is often referred to as the Rape of
Nanjing. But even in the Bible we find such metaphoric language: "You
may enjoy the spoil of your enemies." Rape as a metaphor has been part of
historical accounts and other forms of documentation and depiction of
war for centuries, yet the ways in which rape in war has been analyzed
and understood as a political weapon in conflict settings have been characterized by euphemisms and dismissal.

Marginalizing the phenomenon of wartime rape as a women's problem,
a private problem, or a problem that is too shameful to address has kept
victims and their stories and experiences at arm's length from policy as well
as academic research. As a consequence, we know very little about the ways
in which rape has been used in different wars, why this is the preferred form
of violence in certain settings, how the victims and their societies live with
their experiences after the war has ended, and what political impact these
acts of violence might have during and after a conflict. It is impossible to
address all these issues here, which in any case is not the aim of the present
chapter. Rather, my focus is on mapping out what we know and how we

can find out more by drawing on studies from the wars in the former Yugoslavia.

The Breakup of Yugoslavia and the New Wars

The conflicts that followed the breakup of Yugoslavia marked the beginning of what several scholars have called the "new wars" (Kaldor 1999). Emerging in the aftermath of the Cold War, such new wars are fought within states (Tønnesson 2008), and are characterized by both the absence of legitimate state power (Østerud 2009) and the lack of a clear distinction between civilians and militaries: war and peace are blurred (Kaldor 1999). Whether this type of conflict is actually new or not is open to debate,[1] but both Øyvind Østerud (2009) and Mary Kaldor (1999) agree that the so-called new wars share a common characteristic: they are about identity, and they make identities the front lines of conflict. According to Kaldor (1999), the response to these new wars has been a cosmopolitan effort in which transnational institutions intervene to enforce law and order and police the streets in affected countries.

Helga Hernes (2008, 31) writes that a gender analysis of these new wars shows that "suffering in war is in many ways more gendered than ever before. Women (and civilians more broadly) are forcefully transformed into victims as a consequence of gender-based violence, and by the fact that entire societies collapse and become completely dependent on help from the outside."[2] The Bosnian war (1992–95), the Kosovo conflict (1999), and the international engagement in their aftermaths epitomize these new wars. In both conflicts, rape and sexual violence were documented, prosecuted, and understood in ways never seen before. As international efforts to rectify a history of silence and inaction regarding such crimes intensify—thanks largely to a quartet of UN Security Council resolutions[3]—it remains important to maintain a focus on the early cases of international engagement, that is, Bosnia and Kosovo. What have been the failures, successes, and promises of the concerted international efforts aimed at addressing crimes of sexual violence in the post-Yugoslav wars? Before discussing this in more detail, it will be useful to provide a short overview of the use of sexual violence in the wars in Bosnia and Kosovo,

---

1. Østerud (2009, chap. 2) discusses whether these wars can in fact be called new or simply represent a break with the interstate war pattern and a return to prestate wars.

2. Translated from Norwegian by the author.

3. Specifically, Resolution 1325 (2000), Resolution 1820 (2008), Resolution 1888 (2009), and Resolution 1889 (2009).

along with the shift in international attention and commitment in relation to this issue.

Bosnia

After the secession of Croatia and Slovenia in 1991, followed by that of Bosnia and Herzegovina in 1992, Europe witnessed a level of atrocities that many thought had ended with the Holocaust. The exact number of casualties, refugees, and internally displaced persons will never be known, but it is clear that the Bosnian conflict was the most lethal war on European soil since World War II. The pattern of "ethnic cleansing"—often called a euphemism for genocide—has left wounds and scars that will take generations to heal. An integral part of such ethnic cleansing was the use of sexual violence.

It was after Roy Gutman of *Newsday* reported as early as July 1992 that he had visited a concentration camp in Manjaca in northwestern Bosnia that the use of sexual violence became known among the international public. Gutman had witnessed Muslim prisoners being terrorized by Serb captors (Silber and Little 1995, 249). When he later learned about other concentration camps, among them the notorious death camp Brocko Luka, he discovered that women were also being held as prisoners. Witnesses could tell him that these women had been routinely raped, and a new term was born: "rape camps," which were seen as a version of the concentration camp. Rapes were also documented in the camps in Vogosca, Omarska, and Trnopolje (Gutman 1993, xi). There is some disagreement within the literature over how many rape camps existed in Bosnia—or indeed where they were located. Dan Smith (1997, 34) identifies six such camps—in Brcko, Doboj, Foca, Gorazde, Kalinovik, and Visegrad—that is, mostly in the eastern part of Bosnia. Seada Vranic (1996, 7), on the other hand, while also identifying six rape/death camps, places them mostly in the northern part: in Doboj, Keraterm, Luka near Brcko, Manjaca, Omarska, and Trnopolje. Beverly Allen (1996, 65) explains that restaurants, hotels, hospitals, schools, factories, peacetime brothels, and other buildings served as rape camps, and that the aggressors were mostly Serb personnel from the Yugoslav Army, irregular Serb soldiers, Chetniks (Serb monarchists), and even civilians. But Allen's description captures only part of the picture, because rape occurred on all sides of the conflict. Alexandra Stiglmayer (1994, 115) emphasizes that there exists documentary evidence of rape camps on the Bosnian, Croatian, and Serbian sides alike. However, common to most of the reports she has reviewed concerning these camps is that the available documentation is vague or poor. As soon as particular rape camps were identified, they were dissolved and new ones were established in areas inaccessible to outsiders like the International Red Cross (Stiglmayer 1994, 115). This flux may help explain some of the variation in the documentation of rape camps in Bosnia. In any case, what was described in Bosnian stories of rape seemed to differ from what had been seen in other previous conflicts: the use of sexual violence was reported to be *systematic* and *targeted* against members of different ethnic groups.

Todd Salzman (1998, 356) refers to the so-called RAM plan, which was allegedly developed by Serb army officers in late August 1991. This plan mentions raping women and children as an efficient and integral tool in undertaking the ethnic cleansing of Muslims in Bosnia and Herzegovina. According to a newspaper in Slovenia, the Psychological Operations Department of the Yugoslav National Army believed that the "morale, desire for battle, and will [of Muslims] could be crushed more easily by raping women, especially minors and even children" (quoted in Salzman 1998, 356). RAM means "loom" and is said to refer to the Serb military's policy of weaving its way from many angles across Bosnia and Herzegovina and Croatia (Allen 1996, 58). Salzman therefore concludes that the organized structure of the mass rapes and the rape camps was planned as early as August 1991. This might well be the case, but it explains just part of the picture, because it was not only Serbs who raped Muslims during the four-year war. Three features about the reporting of war rape from the Bosnian conflict set these events apart from rape stories from other conflicts and suggest a change in the ways in which sexual violence in war came to be understood.

First, the introduction of the term "rape camp" into international reporting and documentation suggests that the developments in the Balkans were seen as something other than random acts of violence. It also suggests that the detention/prison settings in which the affected women were held were not primarily designed to get information from the prisoners about male members of their families or other kinds of information that could advance their captors' cause—as was the case in many of the Latin American conflicts during the 1980s and early 1990s. The men and women who were held in detention and suffered various forms of sexual torture were picked out because of their ethnic identities, not because they could provide information. In other words, the rape and sexual violence were quickly seen as an integral part of the ethnic cleansing. The stories about what was happening in Bosnia were uncovered by both local and international journalists only months after the fighting broke out in April 1992.

Second, as a consequence of the organizational and targeted structure mentioned above, the notion of rape being used as a weapon of war in this conflict caught on—both domestically and within the international community. In January 1993, Amnesty International (1993, 4) was among the first organizations to document sexual violence committed in an "organized or systematic way, with the deliberate detention of women for the purpose of rape and sexual abuse." In February of the same year, the European Community (1993, 5) delivered its report to its foreign ministers,[4] in which the number of women raped was estimated at between 10,000 and 60,000, though later reports settled on a figure of 20,000.[5] Alongside these efforts, the United Nations set up its own commission, led by Special Rapporteur of the Commission on Human Rights Tadeusz Mazowiecki, who presented several reports on the human rights situation in the former Yugoslavia. Mazowiecki (1993, para. 85) concluded that rape and sexual violence were clearly used to "humiliate, shame, degrade and terrify the entire ethnic group." In the report cited, Mazowiecki is hesitant to provide a number for how many women were thought to have been raped, but as the quote shows he confirms that the use of sexual violence was seen as systematic, widespread, and intentional. He also expressed great concern in February 1993 that there were too many organizations engaged in too many fact-finding missions, creating a sense among victims of documentation fatigue. While Mazowiecki was still in the initial stages of his work for the United Nations, the Europeans had already delivered their report, alongside those by human rights organizations such as Amnesty International (1993); groups such as the Coordinative Group of Women's Organizations of Bosnia and Herzegovina suggested the number of affected women to be as high as 50,000 (Meznaric 1994),[6] while reports from other individual researchers and networks of nongovernmental organizations (NGOs) estimated that as many as 60,000 women had been raped.[7] The collection and publication of such figures sparked off a chain reaction of hatred and hostility in which Muslims, Croats, and Serbs all took part—and which, in turn, most likely led to more rapes being committed (Nikolic-Ristanovic 1997). The true numbers probably will never be known.

Third, the conflict took place in Europe, among Europeans. While this last point has not been discussed thoroughly in the scholarly literature, and while it cannot be scientifically proven, it is highly likely that the rape

---

4. The report was presented to the UN Security Council at the same time.

5. It is worth noting that these are still the numbers used by most writers on this theme. If this is a good estimate, then it would suggest that most of the rapes happened at the beginning of the war, since these numbers are from just the first year of the conflict.

6. Meznaric (1994) does not comment on the ethnic composition of these totals, however.

7. These figures were presented by Elenor Richter-Lyonette, who works for the Geneva-based NGO Women's Advocacy and was one of the key speakers at the FOKUS (Forum for Women and Development, Norway) seminar held in Oslo on 17 June 1996; she, too, made no comment on the ethnic composition of these figures.

stories were taken more seriously because the Western world identified with the victims they were hearing about. It was not possible to dismiss the stories as concerned with distant cultural traditions or gender relations unfamiliar to the Western world. Rather, the massive documentation and the public exposure of the stories in the international media came from Europeans, which caused us—that is, the Western audience—to listen and to analyze these events in unprecedented ways because the sufferers of these crimes were racially and culturally similar to ourselves—Europeans.

Kosovo

In late March 1999, air forces of the North Atlantic Treaty Organization (NATO) bombed military targets within the Federal Republic of Yugoslavia—that is, targets within the territories of Serbia, Kosovo, and Montenegro. The bombing came as a response to the refusal of Serbian leaders to sign a peace deal with the Albanian population living in Kosovo. About a year prior to these events, the Kosovo Liberation Army (KLA) had declared its aim to achieve its separatist goal by any means necessary. Mass violence erupted, including massacres and systematic use of sexual violence, and thousands of Albanians fled to neighboring countries. The NATO bombing lasted until June 1999, after which Kosovo came under UN administration.

This conflict erupted within three years of the ending of the Bosnian war, and some of the people and groups implicated in the violence during that war again found themselves involved in violent actions, this time in Kosovo. It was therefore not surprising that many people expected sexual violence to be used once again between warring ethnic groups. This time, however, international organizations and NGOs were prepared to address the issue. Some experts in the field who had learned from the Bosnia conflict were sent to the Balkans to establish centers to provide medical and psychosocial help to rape victims. One such organization was Medica Mondiale, an organization based in Germany that had gained a reputation as a resource and therapy center for war-raped women in central Bosnia. In 1998, it transferred some staff from Bosnia to Kosovo, while maintaining its presence in Bosnia.

The political nature of sexual violence in the Balkans was not new. It predates the 1998–99 conflict in Kosovo and the 1992–95 Bosnian war. In the late 1980s, stories emerged of Albanian men raping Serbian women. These stories sparked a massive response by Serbian women, who took to the streets: they demonstrated under the slogans "We are mothers of Serbia" and "We are mothers not whores." The direct trigger for this response was a joke made in October 1987 by Fadil Hoxha, one of the highest-ranking politicians in Kosovo, during a speech at a semiofficial lunch for the reserve military commanders of Kosovo, Serbia, and Montenegro. There, Hoxha had said that "the problem of rapes of Serb women by Albanian men in Kosovo would be solved if more non-Albanian women worked as prostitutes in Kosovo's taverns" (quoted in Zarkov 2007, 21). Dubravka Zarkov (2007) observes that these events showed that ethnicity and gender had become interlinked in ways that further polarized ethnic differences in the region. Like Zarkov, Silva Meznaric (1994, 86) has noted that rape has been used as a means of more starkly drawing lines between ethnic groups in the former Yugoslavia. In particular, she points out that stories of rapes committed against Serbian women led the Republic of Serbia to modify its penal code, and concludes that "sexual assault on citizens of different nationalities and ethnicities was considered more aggravating than 'regular' rape" (Meznaric 1994, 86).

As can be seen, the history of interethnic rape in Kosovo, as well as the knowledge and experiences gained from the Bosnian war, created an international alertness to political rapes in the Kosovo conflict. However, Kosovo was different from Bosnia, and it turned out to be even more challenging to both document and report rapes in Kosovo than it had been in Bosnia. Both Human Rights Watch and the United Nations Population Fund (UNFPA) reported numerous difficulties in documenting the rapes that took place in the province. The Albanian population in Kosovo is seen as more traditional than the populations of other parts of the former Yugoslavia, and this conservatism reduced women's possible avenues—and perhaps also undermined their courage—to come forward and describe the ordeals they had suffered. Mistakes made during the Bosnian conflict—such as a male NGO worker's use of a loudspeaker in a refugee settlement to ask whether any rape victims would like to report their stories (UNFPA 1999, 9)—did not make it easier to reach the women who needed help. Indeed, given the traditional gender roles in the Kosovo region, mistakes of the kind just mentioned as well as others may have simply aggravated the situation. Yet despite the difficulties, many organizations attempted, more or less successfully, to document rape to get the numbers right. One such report was issued in March 2000:

> Human Rights Watch documented 96 cases of rape by Serbian and Yugoslav forces against Kosovar Albanian women immediately before and during the 1999 bombing campaign, and believes that many more incidents of rape have gone unreported. The report said that rapes were not rare and isolated acts committed by individuals, but rather were used deliberately as an instrument to terrorize the civilian population, extort money from families, and push people to flee their homes. Virtually all of the sexual assaults Human Rights Watch has documented were gang rapes involving at least two perpetrators. (Human Rights Watch 2000)

The same report describes how the rapes can be subdivided into three categories: rapes in women's homes, rapes during fighting, and rapes in detention. In addition, it comments on the findings that KLA soldiers committed rapes against Serbian, Albanian, and Roma women in Kosovo after the bombing ended. Rape camps, on the other hand, had not been found, and the authors of the report were critical of the international media for claiming that such camps existed despite the absence of proof. A final but important concern voiced in the report was that the rapes were presented in the media, in reports, and elsewhere in a sensational manner that undermined the victims' right to dignity and privacy. Similar concerns were expressed by Jeanne Ward (2002, 93), and in a report from the Swedish NGO Kvinna til Kvinna (2001, 19) on the situation of women in Kosovo. Researchers from the U.S. Centers for Disease Control and Prevention conducted a survey of 1,358 Kosovar Albanians who had been internally displaced in August and September 1999. They found that the prevalence of rape was about 4 percent (i.e., 4 percent of the people in the sample had experienced rape), while 6 percent had either been raped or witnessed rape. On the basis of these numbers, they suggested that between 23,000 and 45,600 women had been raped between August 1998 and August 1999 (Bastick, Grimm and Kunz 2007, 125).

A conspicuous interpretation of the Kosovo rape stories is that after Bosnia and Rwanda, a large number of international agencies, reporters, NGOs, and others involved in documenting and mapping atrocities in conflict were overeager in their attempts to "get it right"—this time. It appears that there was an almost exaggerated focus on rape and sexual violence, which failed to take into account that the situation in Kosovo was different from the Bosnian setting in both the nature of the conflict and in gender patterns. Further, the events in Kosovo were in no way parallel to those in Rwanda, where rape and sexual violence were an integral part of the genocide. Rather, the Kosovo situation revealed a new pattern in efforts to document violence in war zones: sexual violence had become something that those reporting on war naturally included in their records. The recording was done in ways that were at times sensational, insensitive, and unethical, but the issue had clearly been placed on the agenda.

Ending Impunity

One of the most important responses to the massive documentation of rape and sexual violence in the conflict in Bosnia was a resolve that these acts of violence should not and could not be committed with impunity.[8] The perpetrators had to be brought to justice. Up until the early 1990s, the track record for bringing prosecutions in cases of rape and sexual violence in armed conflicts was unimpressive, to put it mildly. It was therefore imperative that the international response to these events take the form not only of help and assistance to the victims but also of criminal prosecution of the perpetrators at the international level. The international community therefore undertook an unprecedented concerted effort to establish an international criminal prosecution system.

But the path to justice can be difficult at times. The early writings of legal scholars during the Bosnian war addressed some of these difficulties, as they asked how crimes of sexual violence would fit into international criminal law, and when the laws governing war and international crimes could be seen as gender biased. For instance, should sexual violence be analyzed as a crime of gender—that is, as a crime in which women were targeted first and foremost because they were women? Some authors argued that the use of sexual violence in times of war should be seen as a gender or sex crime (Green et al. 1994). Others held that it should be seen as a crime of ethnicity—that is, that women were targeted because they belonged to specific ethnic groups (Cleiren and Tijssen 1994). The archaic language of the legal texts themselves was also identified as a stumbling block. Several authors pointed out the problems involved in associating crimes of sexual violence with the honor of the victims concerned. Rhonda Copelon (1995, 201) explains: "The Geneva Conventions characterize rape as a crime against the honor and dignity of women. . . . Women's 'honor' has traditionally been equated with virginity or chastity. Loss of honor implies the loss of station or respect, reinforcing the social view—often internalized by women—that the raped woman is dishonorable." Such a conceptualization shifts the focus away from the violent acts committed to the chastity of the women concerned. And we might also ask: Who "owns" a woman's honor? Who defines what an "honorable woman" is?

While acknowledging that these difficulties needed to be addressed, in May 1993 the UN Security Council passed Resolution 827, which formally established the International Criminal Tribunal for the Former Yugoslavia (ICTY). This resolution contained the Statute of the ICTY, which set out the tribunal's jurisdiction and organizational structure, as well as the criminal procedure to be followed in general terms. It also recognized rape as an international crime. This date thus marked the

---

8. The similar international response to the atrocities committed during the genocide in Rwanda in 1994 also helped firm this resolve.

beginning of the end of complete impunity for war crimes in the former Yugoslavia. The ICTY was the first war crimes court established by the United Nations, and the first international war crimes tribunal to be set up since the Nuremberg and Tokyo tribunals after World War II. The tribunal is temporary, ad hoc, and has limited jurisdiction—covering the entire territories of the former Yugoslavia, including Croatia, Bosnia and Herzegovina, Kosovo, and Macedonia. The overall aim of the tribunal (together with the International Criminal Tribunal for Rwanda, or ICTR, a similar body set up to deal with crimes committed during the 1994 Rwandan genocide)[9] is to hold major perpetrators accountable for the most serious crimes, although low- and mid-level perpetrators have also been prosecuted (de Brouwer 2005, 15). The court was established in order to address all atrocities committed in the region, but the massive documentation of rape and sexual violence served as an additional impetus for its creation. Since its creation, the ICTY has indicted 162 persons, 58 of whom were inter alia charged with having committed acts of sexual violence (de Brouwer 2005, 18).

When the tribunal terminates its work, criminal prosecutions will be carried out in national courts. The transition from international criminal prosecution to the national level has been taking place since 2004. Judges and other legal personnel have undergone massive training on how to prosecute international crimes, how to provide witnesses with adequate protection, and how to prioritize cases.

In 1998, some years after the establishment of the ad hoc tribunals for the former Yugoslavia and Rwanda, the International Criminal Court (ICC) became a reality. The aim of this court is to prosecute cases that national courts are unable or unwilling to pursue. Article 5 of the Rome Statute of the International Criminal Court lists the crimes that fall within the ICC's jurisdiction, which include only the most serious crimes that are of concern to the international community as a whole—in other words, genocide, crimes against humanity, and crimes of aggression (de Brouwer 2005, 19). With the noteworthy exception of the United States and China, sixty-six countries have ratified the ICC, and the court became a permanent international body on 1 July 2002.

With the ICC in place, a long legal journey of integrating gender concerns within international criminal law has taken a major step forward as an international criminal system that will also prosecute crimes of sexual violence. According to the Coalition of the ICC—a coalition of more than 2,500 organizations working to strengthen international cooperation with the court—the integration of gender into the work of the ICC

---

9. For further information on the International Criminal Tribunal for Rwanda, see www.ictr.org/.

can be seen on different levels. First, at the level of witness protection, the ICC ensures that victims of sexual and gender-based violence will be safe both physically and psychologically, and that their dignity will be safeguarded by being spared harassing and intimidating questions in court. In addition, a trust fund for victims and their families has been set up. Second, at the level of rules of evidence, the court cannot take into account the prior sexual history of a victim as part of the case, nor can it speculate about the consent of the victim, as it recognizes the coercive circumstances of the acts constituting the alleged crime. Third, the staff of the ICC is to include legal advisers who specialize in gender-based crimes, and efforts are to be made to ensure that there is a fair balance between men and women among judges, prosecutors, and registrars. Lastly, the ICC makes provision for women to come forward with their stories without necessarily being witnesses, allowing women's voices to be heard even when regular legal proceedings are not taking place.[10] These policies are clearly based on experiences from the ICTY and the ICTR. In her account of the supranational criminal prosecution of sexual violence, Anne-Marie de Brouwer (2005, 16) writes that "the massive scale of the rapes of women thus proved to be one of the impetuses for setting up an international criminal tribunal that was able to try persons on the basis of individual criminal responsibility. For the first time in history, rape was explicitly recognized to have taken place in an armed conflict and, as such, given explicit standing in the ICTY Statute under Article 5(g) as a crime against humanity." She notes that while the court has had many other charges to investigate beyond the sexual violence crimes, it is also clear that efforts by the ICTY in this field have been setting precedents for future trials and courts.

The ICC Statute specifies particular forms of gender-based crime within international criminal law in ways that are unprecedented. It is now possible to prosecute incidents of rape, sexual slavery, enforced prostitution, forced pregnancy, enforced sterilization, or any other form of sexual violence of comparable gravity as crimes against humanity or war crimes, and a footnote has been added to the 1948 Genocide Conventions to the effect that genocide can include acts of rape and sexual violence (de Brouwer 2005, 20–21). To date, the Office of the Prosecutor is investigating four different situations. The first is in Uganda, where arrest warrants have been issued against the top five leaders of the Lord's Resistance Army, where the charges include crimes of sexual violence. The second is in the Democratic Republic of the Congo (DRC) and involves three

---

10. This section is based on information from the Coalition of the ICC Web page; see www.icc now.org/?mod=gender (accessed 16 September 2009).

cases, with the charges for two of these including crimes of sexual violence. The third is in Sudan and involves three cases, the charges for two of which include crimes of sexual violence—also against children. In addition, one of these cases is against the Sudanese president himself, Omar al Bashir; it also includes counts related to sexual violence as a war crime. The fourth is in the Central African Republic and involves one case in which rape charges are among the counts.

The work carried out in these tribunals shows that the legal conceptualization of crimes of sexual violence during war is evolving and becoming more nuanced with every new verdict. Future cases involving the criminal prosecution of perpetrators of wartime sexual violence will rest on an increasingly elaborate foundation of verdicts and trials, which will, it is hoped, ensure that more offenders will be prosecuted for such crimes.

What more have the criminal prosecutions in the ICTY achieved? The most comprehensive study to date of these cases has been carried out by de Brouwer, who has examined the extent to which the concerns and interests of the victims of sexual violence were integrated into the nascent international law system (2005, 427). Her study shows that it was the ICTY's aim to try between 128 and 138 individuals by the end of 2010, and 58 were expected to be charged inter alia with crimes involving sexual violence (de Brouwer 2005, 331). However, by March 2010, 73 cases involved indictments for crimes of sexual violence.

The result is a wealth of data available for a research community that wants to learn more about the victims and perpetrators of sexual violence in war. Transcripts from the court hearings, videos, and background documents are all available at the ICTY's Web pages (www.icty.org). This massive documentation effort is a gold mine not only for legal scholars but also for social science scholars. Through close examination of these transcripts, it will be possible to critically investigate the question of intent in a social as well as a legal sense.

Perpetrators

The efforts to end impunity, and to bring perpetrators to justice, have also opened up the possibility of studying who these perpetrators are, what motivated them to choose sexual violence over other actions in given settings, and what impact punishment has had both on them and on their victims.

There is now a rich literature on crimes of wartime sexual violence in general, and those committed during the Bosnian conflict in particular, but within these analyses it is predominantly the victims who are given a voice and are being analyzed. The perpetrator is a secondary character whose intentions and motivations are assumed but unexamined. In other words, the ways in which sexual violence in war has been theorized up until now have been based on empirical data from only one of the groups involved in this violent relationship—the victims of such violence. In order to advance our understanding of this area, we need to incorporate empirical data that bring the perceptions and voices of the perpetrators into the equation. This is necessary not to somehow justify the actions of the perpetrators but to seek insights into why and how such behavior can be understood as a social practice in war.

There are several reasons why we need more knowledge about this particular group of perpetrators. On a conceptual level, it seems plausible to assume that there is a difference between the perpetrators of acts of sexual violence in war and those who commit acts of sexual violence in times of peace. This means that the existing body of knowledge on perpetrators of sexual violence might have little applicability to the perpetrators of wartime sexual violence. The setting of war represents an extreme break with the norms and values that guide peaceful coexistence between people(s)—as illustrated by the very fact that killing is permissible under certain conditions in war according to the Geneva Conventions (*jus in bello*). The text on the back cover of a recently published book on Norway's role as an actor on the international military scene states that "the soldier's profession is about being able to kill while risking your own life. The use of military forces in international operations since the end of the Cold War has increased the likelihood that on behalf of Norwegian society at large, Norwegian soldiers will kill other people and suffer losses among their own" (Edström, Lunde, and Matlary 2009).[11] Part of the training that soldiers undergo in regular armies is geared toward learning what actions are permissible under international law given particular sets of circumstances. In other words, soldiers are trained to recognize and analyze in which settings certain forms of violence are legitimized. These settings require clear distinctions to be made between civilians and military personnel, and entail a set of parameters that regulate relationships between military forces on the battleground. When a person in a war situation kills without violating the rules of war, he or she is usually not regarded as a murderer in the aftermath of war, and quite likely will never kill again. Likewise, a perpetrator of sexual violence in war may not be a rapist with a history of offenses involving sexual violence prior to the war, and that violence may have no bearing on behavior after the war. But there is a clear distinction between killing and committing acts of sexual

---

11. Translated from Norwegian by the author.

violence in war: killing can be legitimized under certain conditions, whereas sexual violence cannot. However, it is possible to regard sexual violence in war as part of a repertoire of actions that appear permissible because the circumstances of war are extraordinary and because it elicits no consequences, punishment, or condemnation from the military leadership.

In addition, in the "new wars"—where the front lines are blurred, identities are the battleground, and the distinction between military and civilian is unclear—it is likely that the propensity for extreme violence in all its forms increases just because the opportunity for such violence is present. James Waller (2007, 265) argues that men are implicated in extreme violence more often than women simply because they find themselves more often in situations where such acts can be carried out, and war presents a wealth of such situations. While this may be true, it is also true that many men ignore these opportunities, and it would be interesting to discover when and why some men do and others do not resort to this kind of violence. The information that the research and policy community needs is precisely what happens in the war setting that transforms far too many ordinary men into perpetrators of sexual violence.

This question can be answered by critically examining the contexts in which such acts of violence occur. In his study on how ordinary people commit genocide and mass killing, Waller argues that the

> social construction of cruelty—buttressed by professional socialization, group identification, and binding factors of the group—envelops perpetrators in a social context that encourages and rewards extraordinary evil. It reminds us that the normal reaction to an abnormal situation is abnormal behavior; indeed, normal behavior would be an abnormal reaction to an abnormal situation. We must borrow the perspective of the perpetrators and view their evil not as the work of "lunatics" but as actions with a clear and justified purpose—so defined by a context of cruelty. (Waller 2007, 271)

Maria Eriksson Baaz and Maria Stern (2009) have carried out a study of crimes of sexual violence committed by the Forces Armées de la République Démocratique du Congo (FARDC) in the DRC, focusing on the perpetrators. According to estimates by the UN observer mission in the DRC, the FARDC was responsible for about 40 percent of the sexual violence committed in the first part of 2007 (Baaz and Stern 2009, 497). For their study, the authors interviewed 193 people about the army's use of rape, but did not address whether the interviewees themselves had committed such acts. Instead, the interviews focused on what being a good soldier entailed and how sexual violence intersected with these conceptualizations. What the authors found was that the soldiers conceptualized rape in two distinctly different ways. On the one hand were what the soldiers labeled "lust rapes," which were rapes committed against random women owing to an urge to release sexual tension. The soldiers explained this phenomenon as a consequence of a particular context: their military confinement and the war. Soldiers were uncertain about how long they would be in the military and were both poor and hungry. Such rapes were linked directly to the "poor distribution of resources and organization of the military" (Baaz and Stern 2009, 509), and they were viewed by the interviewees as more ethically palatable than the second kind of rape, which they labeled "evil rapes." These are seen as being part of what Cynthia Enloe (2008, 108) has called the "lootpillageandrape" frenzy: the taking of drugs, the craziness of war, the frustrations and anger of the individual soldier, and the transgressions involved in extreme forms of violence pave the way for the use of sexual violence with no other purpose than the commission of evil acts. Rapes of this type, Baaz and Stern explain, occur in the context of other forms of extreme violence. The aim of their study is to demonstrate that the notion that sexual violence is a weapon of war does little to help us understand the "myriad relations of power which make up the context in which sexual violence occurs" (Baaz and Stern 2009, 514).

These are important insights. They force us to ask new questions about the nature of the context in which war rapes take place and about what the conceptualization of sexual violence as a weapon of war entails. We need to understand the level of this form of violence as well as the reasoning behind its organized nature. For instance, does the sexual violence manifest itself in the form of organized rape camps where acts of sexual violence are targeted and systemic? Who facilitates such setups, and what do the perpetrators know about the arrangements? When and how does the violence take place—in captivity, in a private home, or in public spaces? What rationales lie behind the different contexts? In what contexts are rape and sexual violence rampant but not systematic, and what does that information tell us about the rationale behind such violence and those committing it? In an article that examines the variations in the use of sexual violence in different armed conflicts, Elisabeth Wood (2006) has commented that even in somewhat similar conflicts—such as Sierra Leone and Bosnia, where ethnicity marked the front lines and sexual violence was widespread—the ways in which sexual violence was used varied.[12] In Bosnia, the use of such violence has been documented as systematic and organized, whereas in Sierra Leone it appears to have been the opposite—random and disorganized.

Finally, the perpetrators in question are predominantly soldiers, which calls for an analysis of what military structures "produce" perpetrators of sexual violence. Are such acts of violence most common among paramilitary units with particular ideologies? Is there, for instance, a difference

---

12. See also Wood's chapter in this volume.

between Marxist-based paramilitary units and other paramilitary groups? What about state militaries and private security companies? All these different military constellations will bring individuals—predominantly men— into extraordinary situations, where new codes and norms of behavior will apply. Because their reference group will be other men in the same setting, it is important that we discover more about which of these (close to) all-male military settings appear more conducive to acts of sexual violence than others—and why. A related issue concerns the status, rank, and age of sexually violent offenders. Is it the case that most perpetrators are young recruits? Is the military leadership involved—either by actively encouraging these acts or by knowingly turning a blind eye and a deaf ear to what might be happening under its command?

Emerging Research Themes

Any research agenda on gender and violence must be attuned to future charging gender relations and new forms of violence, which may have different psychological, social, economic, and political outcomes and manifestations. Still, I believe that it is possible to outline a number of issues that require further research.

War children. Twelve years after the Dayton Peace Accords, it is clear that children conceived through the many rapes that took place during the Bosnian war are now reaching an age when they might insist on knowing more about what happened during the war and about their own personal histories. The movie *Grbavica,* which won the Golden Bear at the 2005 Berlin Film Festival, movingly portrays this situation. A casual question to a single mother from her daughter having to do with paying for a school outing, not the war, leads to the uncovering of the mother's rape history. Similar stories are emerging from other sources (e.g., CNN 2007). The status of war children is, at best, underdocumented; at worst, it is simply ignored.[13] In an edited volume focusing on this theme, various authors discuss the legal, social, and ethnic/racial identities of children born to the survivors of wartime sexual violence (Carpenter 2007a). In her introduction, Charli Carpenter (2007b, 2) points out that "to date there have been no systematic fact-finding missions at the global level to assess the need and interests of children born of war in different contexts and to establish best practices with respect to advocating for and securing their human rights."

---

13. Some initiatives exist, such as the Web page www.childrenbornofwar.org/, created by Ingvill Mochmann.

HIV/AIDS and reproductive health. These issues are an integral part of many of the reports and papers on sexual violence in contemporary wars, yet it is clear that they require more research. We need to know more about the extent to which sexual violence in armed conflicts contributes to the spread of HIV/AIDS, both directly and indirectly. There are several interconnecting issues to consider, including the potential secondary stigmatization of having a sexually transmitted disease as well as being a rape victim; the potential ramifications, both symbolic and physical, of the disease for reproductive health; the potential increase in domestic sexual violence following armed conflict; and a potential increase in the sex industry because of difficult economic conditions. In other words, problems associated with HIV/AIDS and reproductive health might increase in tandem with a rise in the use of sexual violence in armed conflict.

Sexualized political discourse. It is also critical to investigate the ways in which political discourse becomes sexualized prior to, during, and after armed conflict. Knowledge of this kind helps us understand how women within different classes, races, and cultures are socially and politically situated in conflicts, and how those differences suggest different levels of vulnerability to sexual violence. An excellent example of this type of study is Zarkov's book (2007) analyzing the conflicts in the former Yugoslavia and exploring how ethnic differences became sexualized as a consequence of a series of events and their coverage by the media in Serbia, Croatia, and Bosnia. This form of analysis is important not only for predicting vulnerability but also for helping us to understand how postwar stigmatization might play out. Drawing on local expertise on gender to enable better understanding of the particulars of gendered norms, roles, and expectations within a given sociopolitical setting would help ensure the best possible research in this field.

Counteracting stigmatization. Building on the former point, there is also a need for studies focusing on social mechanisms that might counteract the stigma attached to having survived sexual violence. Much of the literature is focused on psychosocial help to individual victims, only rarely examining the societal mechanisms that can play an important part in this context. In one such exception, many have mentioned the ways in which Muslim leaders in Bosnia have contributed to lifting the stigma normally attached to rape victims by openly discussing war rape and urging Muslim men not to abandon their respective wives, daughters, or sisters.

Sexual violence against men. Many of the challenges to collecting data on sexual violence in general will also affect any attempt to gather more data on men who are subjected to sexual violence in armed conflict. The documentation of sexual violence against women in war is widely seen as suffering from being anecdotal, but in the case of men the situation is even worse. For better access to data, it might be necessary to involve more men in this research. And organizing psychosocial and medical help in ways that cater to male needs for support would both help the men and make it easier to gather data. At the same time, the most efficient way of reaching female survivors of sexual violence is by offering woman-only help, suggesting serious practical difficulties in reaching both male and female survivors.

In sum, the international engagement in Bosnia and Kosovo regarding crimes of sexual violence was unprecedented. This must be seen as a success. Psychosocial centers were established, reporting was carried out, and impunity was addressed. Nevertheless, all these national and international efforts also reveal the difficulties in addressing the complexity of the phenomenon—including the need to study the perpetrators of such acts, the children born to survivors of wartime sexual violence, and male victims. Further, the individual-based psychotherapeutic help that has been provided has left the potential of societal mechanisms for healing underexplored, and paid insufficient attention to issues regarding the physical health of survivors and the spread of sexually transmitted diseases. While the lack of systematic investigation of these topics persists, the international attention and the Security Council resolutions focusing on the gendered nature of current warfare bodes well for increased research and improved policy responses in the years ahead.

References

Allen, B. 1996. *Rape Warfare: The Hidden Genocide in Bosnia-Herzegovina and Croatia.* Minneapolis: University of Minnesota Press.

Amnesty International. 1993. *Bosnia Herzegovina: Rape and Sexual Abuse by Armed Forces.* AI Index: Eur 63/001/1993. London: Amnesty International.

Baaz, M. E., and M. Stern. 2009. "Why Do Soldiers Rape? Masculinity, Violence and Sexuality in the Armed Forces in the Congo (DRC)." *International Studies Quarterly* 53:495–518.

Bastick, M., K. Grimm, and R. Kunz. 2007. *Sexual Violence in Armed Conflict: Global Overview and Implications for the Security Sector.* Geneva: Geneva Center for the Democratic Control of Armed Forces.

Carpenter, R. C., ed. 2007a. *Born of War: Protecting Children of Sexual Violence Survivors in Conflict Zones.* Bloomfield, CT: Kumarian Press.

Carpenter, R. C. 2007b. "Gender, Ethnicity, and Children's Human Rights: Theorizing Babies Born of Wartime Rape and Sexual Exploitation." In *Born of War: Protecting Children of Sexual Violence Survivors in Conflict Zones,* ed. R. C. Carpenter, 1–20. Bloomfield, CT: Kumarian Press.

Cleiren, C. P. M., and M. E. M. Tijssen. 1994. "Rape and Other Forms of Sexual Assault in the Armed Conflict in the Former Yugoslavia: Legal, Procedural, and Evidentiary Issues." *Criminal Law Forum* 5:471–506.

CNN. 2007. "Children of War." *World's Untold Stories.* CNN.com. March. Available at http://edition.cnn.com/CNNI/Programs/untoldstories/blog/archive/2007_03_18_index.html (accessed 2 July 2010).

Copelon, R. 1995. "Gendered War Crimes: Reconceptualizing Rape in Time of War." In *Women's Rights, Human Rights,* ed. J. Peters and A. Wolper, 197–214. New York: Routledge.

de Brouwer, A.-M. L. M. 2005. *Supranational Criminal Prosecution of Sexual Violence: The ICC and the Practice of the ICTY and the ICTR.* Antwerp: Intersentia.

Edström, H., N. T. Lunde, and J. H. Matlary, eds. 2009. *Krigerkultur i en fredsnasjon* [War Culture in a Peace Nation]. Oslo: Abstrakt.

Enloe, C. 2008. *Globalization and Militarism: Feminists Make the Link.* Lanham, MD: Rowman and Littlefield.

European Community. 1993. "The European Community Investigative Mission into the Treatment of Muslim Women in the Former Yugoslavia: Report to European Community Foreign Ministers." UN Doc. S/25240, Annex I, 3 February.

Green, J., R. Copelon, P. Cotter, and B. Stephens. 1994. "Affecting the Rules for the Prosecution of Rape and Other Gender-Based Violence before the International Criminal Tribunal for the Former Yugoslavia: A Feminist Proposal and Critique." *Hastings Women's Law Journal* 5:171–82.

Gutman, R. 1993. *A Witness to Genocide: The 1993 Pulitzer Prize Winning Dispatches on the "Ethnic Cleansing" of Bosnia.* New York: Macmillan.

Hernes, H. 2008. "De nye krigene i et kjønnsperspektiv" [The New Wars from a Gender Perspective]. In *Kjønn, krig og konflikt* [Gender, War, and Conflict], ed. H. Skjeie, I. Skjelsbæk, and T. L.Tryggestad, 17–32. Oslo: Pax.

Human Rights Watch. 2000. "Serb Gang-Rapes in Kosovo Exposed." 20 March. Available at www.hrw.org/en/news/2000/03/20/serb-gang-rapes-kosovo-exposed (accessed 13 October 2009).

Kaldor, M. 1999. *New and Old Wars: Organized Violence in a Global Era.* Cambridge: Polity Press.

Kvinna til Kvinna. 2001. *Getting It Right? A Gender Approach to UNMIK Administration in Kosovo.* Stockholm: Kvinna til Kvinna.

Mazowiecki, T. 1993. "Situation of Human Rights in the Territory of the Former Yugoslavia: Report on the Situation of Human Rights in the Territory of the Former Yugoslavia Submitted by Mr. Tadeusz Mazowiecki, Special Rapporteur of the Commission on Human Rights, Pursuant to Commission Resolution 1992/S-1/1 of 14 August 1992." UN Doc. E/CN.4/1993/50, 10 February.

Meznaric, S., 1994. "Gender as an Ethno-Marker: Rape, War and Identity in the Former Yugoslavia." In *Identity Politics and Women: Cultural Reassertion and Feminism in International Perspective,* ed. V. M. Moghadam, 76–97. Boulder, CO: Westview.

Nikolic-Ristanovic, V. 1997. "From Sisterhood to Non-Recognition: Instrumentalization of Women's Suffering in the War in the Former Yugoslavia." Paper presented at the conference "Women's Discourses, War Discourses," Ljubljana Graduate School of the Humanities, 2–6 December.

Østerud, Ø. 2009. *Hva er krig?* [What Is War?]. Oslo: Universitetsforlaget.

Salzman, T. A. 1998. "Rape Camps as a Means of Ethnic Cleansing: Religious, Cultural and Ethical Responses to Rape Victims in the Former Yugoslavia." *Human Rights Quarterly* 20:348–78.

Silber, L., and A. Little. 1995. *The Death of Yugoslavia*. Rev. ed. London: Penguin/BBC.

Smith, D. 1997. *The State of War and Peace Atlas*. New rev. 3rd ed. London: Penguin.

Stiglmayer, A. 1994. "The Rapes in Bosnia-Herzegovina." In *Mass Rape: The War against Women in Bosnia-Herzegovina*, ed. A. Stiglmayer, 82–169. Lincoln: University of Nebraska Press.

Tønnesson, S. 2008. "Hva er nytt i krig?" [What Is New in War?]. In *Kjønn, krig og konflikt* [Gender, War, and Conflict], ed. H. Skjeie, I. Skjelsbæk, and T. L. Tryggestad, 127–37. Oslo: Pax.

United Nations Population Fund (UNFPA). 1999. "Assessment Report on Sexual Violence in Kosovo." Mission Completed by D. Serrano Fitamant, Psychology Consultant to UNFPA, 27 April to 8 May 1999, Albania. Available at www.ess.uwe.ac.uk/Kosovo/Kosovo-Current_News196.htm (accessed 18 August 2010).

Vranic, S. 1996. *Breaking the Wall of Silence: The Voices of Raped Bosnia*. Zagreb: Antibarbarus.

Waller, J., 2007. *Becoming Evil: How Ordinary People Commit Genocide and Mass Killing*. Oxford: Oxford University Press.

Ward, J. 2002. *If Not Now, When? Addressing Gender-Based Violence in Refugee, Internally Displaced, and Post-Conflict Settings: A Global Overview*. New York: RHRC Consortium. Available at www.rhrc.org/resources/gbv/ifnotnow.html (accessed 25 May 2010).

Wood, E. J. 2006. "Variation in Sexual Violence during War." *Politics and Society* 34:307–41.

Zarkov, D. 2007. *The Body of War: Media, Ethnicity, and Gender in the Break-up of Yugoslavia*. Durham, NC: Duke University Press.

5

Impact of Violent Conflicts on Women's Economic Opportunities

Tilman Brück and Marc Vothknecht

T he progress of assessing post-conflict recovery has been spurred by two recent developments. First, the importance of economic recovery for the long-term success of peacebuilding efforts in war-torn societies has increasingly been stressed in scholarly and political discourse (e.g., Addison and Brück 2009). Assistance for economic development and for reconstructing livelihoods is crucial to reduce the risk of conflict relapse (Collier and Hoeffler 2004). Second, international agencies and other actors involved in post-conflict reconstruction are paying increasing attention to the different impacts that conflict has on men and women. In this context, UN Security Council Resolution 1325 (2000) was a milestone in addressing gender issues in conflict settings. Underscoring the need for gender mainstreaming in peacebuilding and reconstruction, UNSCR 1325 calls in particular for a greater focus on and involvement of women.

Against that background, the aim of this chapter is to examine the specific economic situation of women in the aftermath of armed conflict. While not minimizing the overwhelming violence and the tremendous pain that both men and women suffer as a result of conflict, our analysis

An earlier version of this chapter was contributed to a United Nations Development Programme publication on post-conflict economic recovery. We gratefully acknowledge helpful comments from the editors of this volume, two referees, and the participants of a UNDP workshop in Greentree in 2007.

85

focuses on the post-conflict economic conditions of women, the constraints they face, the activities they are engaged in, and the well-being they achieve. Given the uniqueness of each conflict and the complexity of women's different experiences in war-affected societies, we aim to identify trends that distinguish women's post-conflict situation both from that of men and from that in nonconflict developing countries.

So far, studies of women's economic situation in the aftermath of war have largely used secondary or anecdotal information or have been based on context-specific anthropological field studies. Reliable data on violent conflict at the individual, household, and group levels are quite rare. This paucity of micro-data seriously hampers researchers' ability to carry out quantitative analysis, especially since gender-disaggregated data are even more scarce (on gender measurement issues, see Moser 2007). This survey aims at bringing together the existing evidence with a particular focus on quantitative results.

We find, first, that women assume a multitude of different roles during and after conflict. Their situation should therefore not be stereotyped, but rather addressed in its full diversity and complexity. Second, violent conflicts affect traditional, prewar gender relations. Conflict and post-conflict developments could accelerate the empowerment of women, conserve the prewar status quo, or reverse progress made toward gender equality.

Third, persistent insecurity and high incidence of domestic violence seem to be decisive factors in the post-conflict rollback of women's wartime gains and the return to prewar gender roles. In periods of reconstruction, post-conflict development activities should therefore assist the permanent transformation of gender roles and in particular address women's access to resources and employment. Fourth, special attention must be paid to the needs of particular vulnerable groups, such as displaced women, female-headed households, female ex-combatants, and the female relatives of male ex-combatants.

Finally, there are still significant knowledge gaps concerning women and postwar reconstruction. More analysis is needed at the micro level—for example, through impact evaluation case studies or household surveys, which are increasingly available from fragile environments. Gender-disaggregated data make possible a better understanding of differences between the sexes in their choices of activity and patterns of employment.

The remainder of the chapter is organized as follows. The basic definitions on which our analysis is based are presented first. We then address, in turn, the qualitative and quantitative evidence on women's post-conflict economic constraints, their choices under these constraints, and their expected welfare outcomes. Finally, the concluding remarks summarize our policy recommendations.

Definitions

Violent Conflict

Violent conflicts share three common characteristics (Berdal and Malone 2000): (1) non-cooperative, destructive, widespread, and persistent action; (2) violation or capture of property rights concerning assets, persons, or institutions; and (3) instigation by some degree of group activity. The type, duration, and intensity of these violent conflicts differ widely, ranging from international wars, civil wars, and genocide to violent protests, riots, coups, revolutions, or terrorism. The relative share of internal conflicts has significantly increased after World War II and the end of colonial times.[1] This shift from interstate to intrastate wars was accompanied by a change in the nature of wars, from conventional battles between armies to the increased involvement and targeting of the civilian population.[2]

The effects of violent conflict on people's economic situation in its aftermath prove to be extremely complex and depend heavily on the conflict, the community, and individual-specific circumstances (Stewart and FitzGerald 2001). In this chapter, we focus on mass violent internal conflicts, which in the past decades have taken place almost exclusively in developing countries, the majority of them in Africa and Asia (Lacina and Gleditsch 2005).

The Post-Conflict Period

"Post-conflict" obviously refers to the aftermath of war. However, the line between active conflict and at least the early post-conflict phase is often ambiguous, as high levels of violence and insecurity often persist even when some form of peace agreement has been reached. Determining the end of a post-conflict period seems to be still more challenging: sometimes, the holding of free elections is judged as a major step to normalization and a peaceful future development.

---

1. Between 1945 and 1999, about 120 civil wars that killed at least 1,000 persons occurred in a total of 73 states (Fearon and Laitin 2001).

2. It is often said that up to 90 percent of the casualties in today's wars are civilians (see, e.g., Sivard 1996). However, Lacina and Gleditsch (2005) question this figure and point to the lack of adequate data on war-related deaths. Their estimates for the percentage of nonbattle deaths in nine selected conflicts in Africa range between 71 and 98 percent.

Unsolved underlying causes of conflict, new tensions provoked by peace accords, weak state institutions, or economic destitution, however, may each or in combination spur a return to armed hostilities. In fact, the risk of conflict relapse is especially high within five years of the end of a previous conflict.[3] The duration of post-conflict periods thus cannot be specified with precision and depends heavily on both the specific conflict setting and individual perception. Being aware of this, we refer to the first decade following the end of war as the limit of the post-conflict era.

Gender

Gender is defined in many different ways in the literature. Though it is often conflated with biological sex, a more holistic approach is required to conceptualize it appropriately. According to Richard Strickland and Nata Duvvury (2003, 5), "gender is determined by the composite of shared expectations and norms within a society concerning appropriate female and male behaviors, characteristics, and roles. Gender and gender roles are culturally specific, learned, changeable over time, and influenced by variables such as age, race, class, and ethnicity."

Such gender roles both influence and are shaped by episodes of violent conflict. In recent years, the specific situation of men in wartime has also started to receive attention in the scholarly discourse. Sarah Martin (2005), for instance, analyzes the masculine culture within peacekeeping missions and discusses ways to address the problem of sexual exploitation and abuse by armed forces; Rosemary Jaji (2009) describes the struggles of young refugee men in Kenya when their notions of masculinity are challenged in exile. More research is needed to better understand how violence and insecurity affect the distinct gender roles and the relations between the sexes.

In this chapter, we focus explicitly on the fate of women and girls in war and postwar situations. Over the course of the past decade, the specific vulnerabilities and needs of women have increasingly been considered by peacebuilding policies and programs. The 1995 Fourth World Conference on Women in Beijing identified the effects of armed or other kinds of conflict on women as one of the critical areas of concern. In 2000, this concern finally resulted in UNSCR 1325, which recognizes the need for gender mainstreaming in all elements of peacebuilding and reconstruction and addresses in particular the impact of conflict on women. Major international agencies engaged in conflict areas, such as the World Bank and the United Nations Development Programme (UNDP), have

---

3. Chalmers (2007), for example, finds a 44 percent probability of recurrence within five years of the end of a previous conflict.

since included gender perspectives in their analytical frameworks (see, e.g., Bouta, Frerks, and Bannon 2005 for the World Bank; UNDP 2003).

Socio-economic Contexts Before, During, and After War

In this chapter, we want to shed light on the specific situations of women who remained in their home communities, female ex-combatants, refugees, female-headed households, and girls of school age. Our unit of analysis is therefore the individual and, at times, the household. Drawing on recent evidence from the micro level, we aim at compiling a comprehensive picture of the economic circumstances typically faced by women during and after war.

While qualitative work offers in-depth insights into particular aspects of a certain conflict and provides valuable information on the underlying dynamics of conflict, (micro-)econometric studies can build on and add to this process through the analysis of more general trends and interrelations. Large nationwide surveys, for instance, make it possible to detect age, gender, or regional differences that are difficult to assess with small samples. We therefore focus in particular on recent results from the relatively young field of quantitative conflict studies.

Our review of the literature is augmented with an overview of basic development indicators from war-torn and peaceful societies, in order to illustrate some general conditions and trends. Table 1 presents a range of socioeconomic figures from developing countries;[4] we distinguish countries not affected by conflict, countries currently at war, and "postwar" countries where the most recent war has ended less than ten years ago.[5]

In table 1, mean values by war status are presented for the time period 1980–2004. We restrict the analysis to developing countries in order to obtain a rather homogenous and hence comparable sample. Still, this type of analysis has some limitations. First, information is not available from all countries, and this deficiency is likely to result in an attenuation bias— that is, an underestimation of effects wherever data from the most war-torn areas are least complete. Second, no causal relationships from war to development can be inferred from such comparisons.

---

4. We use the country classification proposed by the World Bank (http://go.worldbank.org/D7SN0B8YU0). We classify low-income and lower-middle-income economies as "developing," while upper-middle-income and high-income economies are "developed."

5. Information on violent conflict is taken from the UCDP/PRIO Armed Conflict Dataset Codebook Version 4-20075 (see Gleditsch et al. 2002). For the purposes of this study, we focus on (civil) wars—i.e., wars in which 1,000+ battle deaths are observed in at least one year during the course of the conflict.

Table 1. Development Indicators by War Status (1980–2004)

Indicator	Mean value			Mean difference relative to peacetime	
	Peace	War	Postwar	Wartime	Postwar
A. Macro Indicators					
GDP per capita, PPP	2,189	2,366	2,645	8%	21%
GDP growth (annual %)	9.9	1.6	6.7	−45%	134%
Military expenditure (% of GDP)	2.1	3.2	2.4	50%	14%
Agriculture, value added (% of GDP)	27.3	31.9	27.0	17%	−1%
B. Labor Market					
Unemployment, female (% of female labor force)	12.3	11.9	11.4	−4%	−7%
Unemployment, total (% of total labor force)	9.1	9.4	9.2	4%	1%
Employees, agriculture, female (% of female employment)	32.0	27.6	37.4	−14%	17%
Employees, services, female (% of female employment)	52.7	55.5	48.2	5%	−8%
C. Health					
Life expectancy at birth, female (years)	60.3	59.7	62.7	−1%	4%
Life expectancy at birth, male (years)	56.4	55.8	58.4	−1%	4%
Fertility rate, total (births per woman)	4.6	4.8	4.4	4%	−6%
Immunization, measles (% of children ages 12–23 months)	65.9	57.2	71.4	−13%	8%
Prevalence of undernourishment (% of population)	24.6	27.3	27.3	11%	11%
D. Education					
Public spending on education, total (% of GDP)	4.5	3.5	3.1	−24%	−32%
Ratio of girls to boys in primary and secondary education (%)	92.1	89.2	89.3	−3%	−3%
School enrollment, secondary, female (% gross)	49.4	42.2	51.0	−15%	3%
School enrollment, secondary, male (% gross)	51.6	45.9	56.8	−11%	10%
Number of country-year observations[†]	3,142	587	286		

Source: World Development Indicators 2008. Available at http://data.worldbank.org/data-catalog/world-development-indicators/wdi-2008 (accessed 26 August 2010)

"War" and "postwar" are defined according to the UCDP/PRIO War dataset (see Gleditsch et al. 2002); PPP = purchasing power parity. Countries included are categorized as low-income or lower-middle-income economies by the World Bank.

[†]Subject to data availability for each indicator.

Despite these caveats, the figures provide some interesting impressions of the situation in war-affected countries and supplement our survey of existing micro evidence. In table 2, the same exercise is repeated separately for developing countries from Africa, Latin America, and Asia, in order to reveal potential differences across regions. We will refer to these cross-national descriptors throughout the chapter.

Constraints on Economic Opportunities

The constraints to women's economic empowerment, especially in war-torn societies, are manifold and are important determinants of their choices of activity and welfare outcomes. In this section, we look briefly at the prewar situation of women and at possible changes in gender roles caused by violent conflict, then examine the existing evidence on obstacles to women's economic participation during the post-conflict period.

Prewar Situation of Women

Laws, cultural norms, customs, family traditions, and religious practices may all interfere with women's economic opportunities. This is particularly true for developing countries, where the vast majority of violent internal conflicts after World War II have taken place. Because heavily patriarchal structures are dominant in most of these societies, some general features of women's situation prior to conflict can be identified.

Economic participation is often seen as one of the key factors to empower women on the way to more gender equality. However, women's employment opportunities are often hampered by traditional legislation and sociocultural customs (Jütting et al. 2006). In many developing countries, the primary sector is still dominant and most rural households are engaged in agriculture, with the work patterns of women differing markedly from those of men.

Women are generally responsible for domestic work and, in addition to their unpaid household and caregiving responsibilities, are often engaged in activities in the informal sector: even when women working in agriculture (often as unpaid workers on the family farm) are excluded, more than 60 percent of women workers in developing countries are employed informally (Chen et al. 2005). This significant lack of access to formal employment for women can be traced back to gender disparities in other areas.

First, in many developing countries, social institutions limit women's access to resources such as education or health care. Education, though, is crucial to their empowerment: educated women marry later, have fewer and healthier children, know their rights better, and have much higher chances of gaining formal employment. Moreover, a mother's education

Table 2. Development and War by Continent (1980–2004)

Indicator	Africa Peace (Avg.)	Africa Δ War	Africa Δ Postwar	Latin America Peace (Avg.)	Latin America Δ War	Latin America Δ Postwar	Asia Peace (Avg.)	Asia Δ War	Asia Δ Postwar
A. Macro Indicators									
GDP per capita, PPP	1,710	−30%	−43%	3,447	32%	23%	1,941	24%	62%
GDP growth (annual %)	2.9	−71%	179%	2.2	−31%	65%	5.8	−18%	−16%
Military expenditure (% of GDP)	2.3	84%	22%	1.3	71%	−8%	2.3	6%	59%
Agriculture, value added (% of GDP)	28.3	51%	38%	19.9	−15%	−14%	29.3	−14%	−26%
B. Labor Market									
Unemployment, female (% of female labor force)	16.8	16%	12%	11.4	3%	−16%	4.7	130%	115%
Unemployment, total (% of total labor force)	11.7	39%	24%	8.7	9%	6%	3.4	142%	79%
Employees, agriculture, female (% of female employment)	40.8	17%		6.8	−52%	−11%	55.7	−23%	12%
Employees, services, female (% of female employment)	48.7	−25%		75.7	1%	−2%	27.1	56%	−10%

C. Health

Life expectancy at birth, female (years)	54.7	-8%	-6%	67.0	2%	6%	64.3	-1%	-3%
Life expectancy at birth, male (years)	51.9	-9%	-7%	62.1	-1%	4%	61.1	0%	-2%
Fertility rate, total (births per woman)	5.7	7%	7%	4.0	2%	-6%	3.5	18%	24%
Immunization, measles (% of children ages 12–23 months)	61.5	-15%	2%	65.8	-10%	28%	63.9	-4%	-1%
Prevalence of undernourishment (% of population)	27.2	27%	37%	22.8	-11%	-13%	25.6	-10%	-20%

D. Education

Public spending on education, total (% of GDP)	4.8	-18%	-9%	4.4	-16%	-36%	3.5	-16%	-21%
Ratio of girls to boys in primary and secondary education (%)	86.7	-2%	-10%	100.9	2%	-5%	95.3	-6%	-9%
School enrollment, secondary, female (% gross)	32.4	-29%	-52%	68.9	1%	-16%	56.3	-8%	-24%
School enrollment, secondary, male (% gross)	37.1	-27%	-42%	64.9	1%	-7%	57.6	1%	-9%

PPP = purchasing power parity.

Source: World Development Indicators 2008. Available at http://data.worldbank.org/data-catalog/world-development-indicators/wdi-2008 (accessed 26 August 2010)
No figure is reported for the post-conflict period for Africa, as too few observations are available from post-conflict settings.

also has a positive impact on her children's educational attainment and thus has long-term, transgenerational effects (Klasen 2002). Today, female school enrollment rates in developing countries are, on average, still lower than those of males (see table 1, panel D). In some regions, most notably in southern and western Asia as well as in sub-Saharan Africa, this gender-based discrimination in access to education is particularly prevalent (United Nations 2006; see table 2, panel D). As a result of the low educational attainment of women, girls' future employment and economic prospects are limited.

Second, in many developing regions women's economic opportunities are restricted by legal frameworks and customary law. Laws often constrict women's ownership rights and limit their access to credit or their right to acquire and own land. Inheritance laws as well favor men in many developing countries (Jütting et al. 2006). Even if laws mandating gender equality are on the books, enforcement mechanisms are often insufficient, and traditional, gender-discriminating customs are likely to prevail.

Third, women are often discriminated against in access to formal employment. Even when they possess the same skills as men, women are less likely to be employed, due either to legislative constraints or to prejudices against women working. The higher average unemployment rates among women that we observe in the developing world (see table 1, panel B) might also be driven by such discriminatory practices.

Fourth, systemic inequality between men and women also persists in access to political participation. Progress in enhancing women's representation has been steady but slow; on average, women make up 18 percent of the world's national legislatures. Regional differences are thus substantial, and the lowest rates of female delegates are found in the Arab world. But some impressive gains have been registered in recent elections—for example, in Rwanda and Angola (Inter-Parliamentary Union 2009). We expect that women's interests are seldom taken into account and that existing gender inequalities are perpetuated or even worsened when female participation in decision making and leadership is low.

Women's Roles during Conflict

Depending on the specific circumstances of the conflict, women play a multitude of different roles: not solely as passive victims but also as active participants, either in war or in the organization of life in their home communities. During conflict, traditional gender roles are therefore likely to shift.

WOMEN AT HOME

In times of conflict, while men leave home to engage in war, women normally remain in place to tend to the family. In addition to their prewar duties, during this time women increasingly assume tasks traditionally assigned to men, including earning cash income (Bop 2001). This extra burden that women have to bear also constitutes an opportunity to assume new responsibilities, to acquire new skills, to run new businesses, and to gain self-esteem from these activities. Cross-country comparisons support this tendency: on average, we observe slightly lower rates of female unemployment in war-affected economies as compared to countries not at war, while overall unemployment tends to increase in wartime (see table 1, panel B).

Women's adoption of more proactive roles during conflict is not limited to the domestic sphere; it can also be observed in decision-making processes, primarily at the local level. In the absence of men, women organize more aspects of community life and try to maintain basic social services. Thus, while many women's exposure to brutal violence during conflict must not be disregarded, this situation may also generate new opportunities and offer a possible route to their long-term empowerment.

Displaced People

The changing nature of civil wars in the past decades, and the increase attacks on civilians has led to drastic expansion of the displaced and refugee population.[6] Depending on the nature of the conflict and on local conditions, families flee either prior to or after an attack has taken place. With a large proportion of men involved in fighting, these displaced families are often headed by women, have above-average dependency ratios, and exhibit special needs once the conflict is over. However, life in refugee camps also changes gender roles and offers new responsibilities and economic opportunities to women, who may create networks of survival, acquire new skills, and become more self-confident in a setting in which patriarchal control is relatively weak (Meintjes 2001).

War Participants

Women often also participate actively in war and may assume a multitude of different roles, from combatants to spies, logistical supporters (for example, cooks or nurses), or forced sexual partners. Women's reasons to participate are thus as varied as those of men: the military provides female combatants with employment, and in some cases women even benefit from educational opportunities when offered training in logistical or administrative areas (Meintjes 2001). In wars seeking to liberalize a society, for

---

6. By the end of 2006, more than 12 million refugees and asylum seekers worldwide had left their countries of origin (USCRI 2006), and 23.7 million internally displaced persons in more than fifty countries were forced to migrate within national boundaries (IDMC 2006).

instance, women may well embrace the war's objectives. More often, however, their participation is due to military force or economic necessity.

IMPACT ON GIRLS

An ongoing war affects all areas of life, including the education of children. Male and especially female enrollment rates in secondary education seem to decrease substantially, particularly during conflicts on the African continent (see tables 1 and 2, panel D). Girls may be taken away from school by their families for security reasons. During conflicts, older children may also have to enter the workforce to replace adult males. Factors that impede the continuity of schooling during conflict are the destruction of educational infrastructure, the absence of teachers, and often a significant decrease in government spending on education (Stewart and Fitz-Gerald 2001). But even if schooling can be sustained, parents often decide to keep their daughters at home to protect them from violence, sexual abuse, and the risk of being taken hostage on their way to or even at school. Finally, while concerns about forced military recruitment often focus solely on boys, girl soldiers play an important role in many conflicts and the threat to them as well has been increasingly acknowledged in recent years (Fox 2004).

Women's Constraints in the Aftermath of Conflict

When armed conflict ends, many of the difficulties that arose during war do not disappear; in fact, new challenges often emerge. The breakdown of the rule of law, a vacuum of political power, and the destruction of physical infrastructure, social services, and trust throughout the society, as well as a general lack of economic opportunities, all constitute huge obstacles to the reconstruction of a peaceful society and to economic recovery.

Widespread possession of arms and ammunition (mainly among ex-combatants), combined with the absence of an effective police force, often creates an extremely insecure environment (see, e.g., Small Arms Survey 2005, chap. 10). Ex-combatants, other war participants, refugees, and internally displaced people need to be reintegrated into society. For the society affected, all these tasks pose huge challenges that are often insurmountable without international aid.

Male-dominated societies tend to again allocate roles in traditional ways, and prewar constraints on women's potential for economic development often persist in the aftermath of armed conflict. The (re)formation of national identities, associated gender expectations, and the post-conflict return to what is considered "normal" in mostly patriarchal societies leave little room for women's empowerment (Handrahan 2004). When returning men attempt to reassert their claims, the new roles and responsibilities of women, and thus the chance of permanent transformations that bring women closer to equality and autonomy, are put at risk.

The persistence of high levels of violence seems to be one factor in this rollback of women's wartime gains. In the transition from war to peace, women are often particularly vulnerable to physical and sexual abuse. Gender-based violence seems to shift from the public to the private sphere, and the primary perpetrators are no longer rebels or members of the armed forces but family members. Recent studies and information gathered by organizations operating in post-conflict settings confirm that domestic violence increases in the aftermath of conflict: these reports come from various countries, including East Timor (UNTAET 2002), Liberia, and Burundi (Couldrey and Morris 2007). Lina Abirafeh (2007) assesses the increasing gender-based violence in post-Taliban Afghanistan and stresses the difficulties in obtaining reliable information.

That levels of violence remain high or even rise in post-conflict times can often be blamed in part on security forces that are inadequate or even actively involved (Neild 2001). More generally, weak state and societal institutions in prewar times tend to persist into the recovery period and are likely to continue to shape gender relations once the conflict ends. Though difficult to distinguish, the effects of war should therefore not be confounded with those attributable to underlying structural characteristics of the society.

Given this framework, we look at specific situations of women in the wake of war and try to identify some basic patterns. The quantitative evidence on women's postwar situation and on conflict-induced changes in gender roles is generally scarce. The Organization for Economic Cooperation and Development has recently begun compiling the Gender, Institutions and Development Database to provide information on social institutions at a national level (Jütting et al. 2006). Unfortunately, because the database is so new, it does not yet support the comparisons needed to assess changes in these institutions during and after violent conflict.

At the micro level, little gender-disaggregated information is available from conflict-affected regions, and the scale and impact of gender-discriminating practices often remain unclear. Changes of gender roles as a result of conflict, for example, are amply described in qualitative empirical case studies (see, e.g., Rubio-Marín 2006), but quantitative evidence is still scarce. The following presents both evidence from qualitative case studies and reports from policy-oriented organizations active in conflict areas, as well as the existing quantitative evidence on the constraints faced by different groups of women in the aftermath of war.

FEMALE-HEADED HOUSEHOLDS

The share of single women who have lost their partners during conflict typically rises significantly in war-affected societies. Depending on its duration and intensity, violent conflict usually causes major demographic changes because of the particularly high death toll among young men and the resulting increases in female:male ratios, the number of female-headed households, and dependency ratios. Quan Li and Ming Wen (2005) empirically analyze the impact of armed conflict on adult mortality and find higher immediate mortality rates among men in intrastate conflicts (though in the long run women's mortality attributable to war seems to be as high as men's, owing to the conflict's lingering effects).

In the overall difficult economic situation after violent conflict, single women frequently also have to deal with gender-specific constraints on economic development (Brück and Schindler 2009a). A major obstacle is their often-limited right to own land and other property, which is of particular importance for the majority of rural households whose livelihoods depend on agricultural activities. Analyzing the determinants of the area cultivated by farm households in northern Mozambique after the civil war, Tilman Brück and Kati Schindler (2009b) find that female-headed households suffer severe land constraints, even after observable differences in their asset endowments and skills are controlled for and even in regions where land is relatively abundant. Similar results are revealed by the analysis of a small but unique set of panel data that followed the same Rwandan households before and after the 1994 genocide: Patricia Justino and Philip Verwimp (2006) find that the loss of land was a major obstacle to their movement out of poverty and a key reason that female-headed households fell into poverty, mostly because of the transfer of land to a son or the need to sell the land for economic reasons.

Aside from their access to land, women's access to credit, as well as to courses imparting basic business and management skills, is often limited (Sørensen 1998). Moreover, women's responsibilities to provide care for dependent or disabled family members and a lack of child-care facilities often further hamper their possibilities to generate income (De Watteville 2002).

DISPLACED PEOPLE

Gains that women may have achieved in refugee camps are at risk in the aftermath of war, as new social relationships, tasks, and responsibilities are likely to be lost in the process of repatriation. Refugees coming home often face obstacles similar to those of ex-combatants: upon their return, neighbors are suspicious of the returnees' behavior and new skills acquired during conflict.

These issues are particularly acute for women. In many cases, they are expected to adopt traditional, prewar roles in order to achieve community acceptance (see, e.g., Preston 1994 for Namibia; Watson 1996 for Chad). Women therefore may decide either to remain in exile or to move to more urban areas, where they hope to find greater chances of economic independence. However, the possible barriers to women's economic empowerment (most notably, their lack of skills, resources, and social networks) may be even higher in the highly competitive urban environment.

Some quantitative evidence is available for Colombia: using data on more than 2,300 displaced households in twenty-one Colombian departments, Ana María Ibáñez and Andrés Moya (2006) show that displaced households suffered significant losses of assets as a consequence of forced migration; largely from rural areas, they had major difficulty in finding employment in urban labor markets, because their levels of skill and education were usually low. Moreover, both their access to informal credits from relatives, neighbors, and friends and their participation in formal social networks dropped significantly, impairing the ability of the often female-headed households (37 percent of the whole sample) to mitigate risks and to smooth consumption.

War Participants

Female ex-combatants and other women who have been involved in war activities are likely to face particular difficulties in social reintegration. On returning home, female ex-combatants may be stigmatized by their communities both for participating in the destructive processes of war and for abandoning their traditional gender roles. The returnees often find it difficult to reassume their prewar status in the domestic sphere after having experienced different roles during war. Given that most ex-fighters have low levels of education and few vocational skills, their access to formal employment is extremely limited, and the prejudices of private employers against hiring female ex-combatants make matters worse. In the past, "disarmament, demobilization, and reintegration" (DDR) programs have often focused on (male) ex-combatants and therefore did not pay attention to those women who participated in war as unofficial auxiliaries performing noncombat tasks (Greenberg et al. 1997).

In short, enduring social norms, high levels of gender-based violence (particularly in the domestic sphere), and the resulting pressure to resume prewar domestic roles seriously constrain women's attempts to achieve prosperity in post-conflict societies. The return of male ex-combatants to local employment markets, discrimination in access to resources, and a lack of child-care facilities further impair the prospects for women's economic participation.

Limited Economic Choices

Women's economic opportunities in the wake of war are determined by both individual characteristics and conflict-specific circumstances. As a general rule, the harsh economic conditions and the increasing share of single women and female-headed households in post-conflict societies seem to boost women's participation in the labor force.

A study of six countries emerging from armed conflict (Bosnia and Herzegovina, Cambodia, El Salvador, Georgia, Guatemala, and Rwanda), for instance, found an increase in female labor force participation in all six countries (Kumar 2001). Given the constraints previously outlined, women's economic and employment opportunities in both agriculture and the formal sector may become worse in post-conflict times, likely resulting in a "feminization" of informal employment (Bouta, Frerks, and Bannon 2005).

Agricultural Activities

The recovery of the primary sector is often impeded by the war-related destruction of essential infrastructure, the contamination of cultivable land with land mines, a lack of farming equipment, or ongoing displacement. Farm households' choices of war and postwar activity are therefore remarkably different from those in peacetime. Prevailing insecurity and violence in the wake of war may block farmers' access to markets and thus thwart their efforts to gain from market exchange.

Klaus Deininger (2003) shows that the persistent civil strife in Uganda during the 1990s reduced off-farm investments and led to a shift of economic activities toward subsistence and away from market integration. Similarly, agricultural households in Rwanda generally tended to return to subsistence farming after the 1994 genocide, and the poorest households, often headed by females, concentrated mainly on the production of core staple foods (McKay and Loveridge 2005).

Women often encounter specific difficulties in cultivating their land, particularly in the absence of their husbands or male relatives. Customary inheritance and property laws often limit women's access to land, especially when usable land is scarce and claimed by both residents and returnees. In addition, the disappearance of social networks and the lack of cash to hire workers often results in a shortage of the farm labor necessary to cultivate the land (Brück and Schindler 2009b).

Marijke Verpoorten (2009) shows that the Rwandan households most affected by violence were prevented from selling their cattle (the usual response to economic stress), because roads were unsafe and thus markets were inaccessible. Using data from rural Burundi, Tom Bundervoet (2007) investigates the impact of violent conflict on the relationship between savings (here, the accumulation of livestock) and choices of how to act (here, whether to adopt risky or nonrisky crops). He finds, as expected, that more accumulated livestock, which serves as security, increases the probability of choosing to embark on more risky, higher-value activities. However, those households living in regions most affected by violent conflict seemed to assume that their assets are at higher risk and therefore continue to cultivate low-risk crops. In addition, female-headed households invested more in low-risk crops than the male-headed ones, a decision that points to their particular vulnerability.

The same is observed by Brück (2004a) for postwar rural farm households in northern Mozambique: in general, only a relatively small fraction of total income came from the crop market, and the proportion of pure subsistence households increased in the post-conflict period observed. Households with a higher dependency ratio were far less likely to participate in the crop market, while market participation increased as household human capital rose. Female-headed households on average had a significantly higher share of subsistence income than did other households.

Poor households near the absolute survival threshold were likely to adopt very risky coping strategies that increased their already high vulnerability. Primarily because of the war-induced destruction of alternative options, these households specialized in fewer activities and reduced their asset base to nothing in order to secure survival. Finally, village-level features, such as the existing infrastructure, were important determinants of coping strategies. The provision of public goods and the reduction of war-induced transaction costs enhanced both market participation and opportunities for diversification.

Farm households in post-conflict settings, especially households headed by females, are thus likely to adopt inefficient agricultural practices, often return to subsistence production, and are in some cases forced to sell their assets to secure survival—all choices that tend to reinforce their vulnerability and their exposure to chronic poverty risks. In this situation, women in many post-conflict places establish self-help organizations to aid them in demanding equal property rights, mobilizing resources, and furthering agricultural production (Sørensen 1998).

Nonagricultural Activities

Offering a regular income as well as relative job security, employment in the formal sector is in great demand, though it is also often extremely scarce in the aftermath of war. While private sector activities and public services often shut down during fighting, the economy usually tends to expand in the post-conflict period (above-average GDP growth in the recovery period is observed across world regions; see table 2, panel A), mostly triggered by reconstruction activities and the need of an often large international community on the ground for local staff.

Women's access to formal employment depends on the specific post-conflict circumstances. Women with jobs might lose them to returning men, because priority is given to male employment, and women are expected to resume their prewar domestic roles. Women's responsibility for parenting and the absence of child-care facilities further contribute to their economic marginalization. And many women find that their low levels of skills, experience, and formal education make employment in the industrial and service sectors highly unlikely.

In some cases, however, the post-conflict needs for human resources encourage female participation in the labor force, even when it challenges the existing gender roles. The post-conflict era may provide new fields of employment for women: they may possess new skills acquired in jobs during conflict, which they may be able to retain in the post-conflict period (Kumar 2001, 22–24). Further, they may gain job opportunities that result from the presence of international organizations or from the recovery of sectors—such as education, health, or tourism—that traditionally employ women.

Still, female access to formal employment often remains extremely limited and many women rely on activities in the informal sector, which are difficult to capture in official statistics. The varied range of women's informal business activities—most of which are based on trade—is impressive. Often undertaking these income-generating activities in times of war, women engage in petty trade, create networks to transfer money and goods, and, in this way, are able to acquire business and management skills (see, e.g., Chingono 1996 for Mozambique). Other informal coping strategies of women in war-torn societies include small-scale business activities, such as peddling or the selling of cooked food and home-brewed beer (Sørensen 1998). Women may also rely on their domestic skills to find work as maids, while casual agricultural labor offers employment in rural areas.

On the one hand, activities in the informal sector provide a valuable means of earning a living, as neither access to land nor large investments are required to start such a business, and the time between initial investment and return is usually quite short. But on the other hand, the scope and success of their informal activities are often limited by their lack of access to credit, insufficient business skills, and paucity of support from family and social services for help with child care.

Economic destitution may also force women to engage in illegal activities, such as smuggling. Women who migrate to urban areas are at particular risk of ending up in prostitution, which becomes a growing source of income in conflict-affected societies and is often further promoted by the arrival of international aid staff (UN OCHA/IRIN 2007). When earnings are low and unstable, women are also likely to rely on several income sources to provide for their families.

Data, and hence quantitative evidence on female participation in the labor market in war-affected countries, are quite scarce, however. Cross-national comparisons indicate a relatively lower proportion of women employed in agriculture in war-affected countries, probably driven by a relatively higher female involvement in service sector activities, while this trend is apparently reversed in post-conflict times (see table 1, panel B). This pattern is particularly clear on the Asian continent. In Africa, in contrast, the share of women employed in the primary sector is on average higher during war, while relatively fewer women are engaged in the (formal) service sector in wartime (see table 2, panel B). Generally, these figures are based on few observations, which are especially scarce from the most severely affected regions and should therefore not be overinterpreted.

Some case study evidence is available: using two national household surveys from early and late postwar Mozambique, Tilman Brück and Katleen Van den Broeck (2006) assess the impact of individual and household characteristics on the type of employment. They find that men are much more likely than women to earn an income both in agriculture and in the nonagricultural sector, either through self-employment or as wage workers. Especially in rural areas, women have a high probability of helping in other household members' activities without receiving a monetary income.

Florence Kondylis (2010) analyzes labor market patterns in postwar Bosnia and Herzegovina and finds displaced individuals substantially less likely to be working than the people who stayed. While this translates to higher unemployment—that is, an active search for work—among men, women tend to drop out of the formal labor force, either to find work within the informal sector or to devote themselves to household production.

In sum, most women in post-conflict settings are likely to have only limited choices as to participating in the economy and generating income. The disadvantages and discrimination they suffer in the formal labor markets, as well as their restricted access—especially for single women—to agricultural land and livelihoods, often result in increased rates of female participation in the informal sector.

Impact of War on Women's Welfare

The assessment of the impact of violent conflict on women's welfare must focus not only on measures of income or consumption but also on health outcomes and education.

Income and Consumption

The livelihoods of rural households may be especially affected when agricultural production becomes impossible in the wake of war. When access to cultivable land is allowed, (the return to) subsistence farming often enhances the welfare of the household and guarantees the survival of its members. Depending on the cultural context, households headed by females might be particularly vulnerable to the loss of their land and the risk of extreme destitution.

A relatively large body of literature has proven the post-conflict vulnerability of female-headed households. Marijke Verpoorten and Lode Berlage (2007) as well as Justino and Verwimp (2006) find that in the aftermath of the Rwandan genocide, female-headed households are more likely to be poor and less likely to move out of poverty. Bundervoet (2006) evaluates absolute consumption poverty in postwar rural Burundi and shows that households headed by females are much more vulnerable to poverty, while landownership has had a strong poverty-reducing effect.

Similarly, postwar income and consumption levels of households headed by females in rural northern Mozambique were far lower than expected, even when household and local (village/land/social institutions) characteristics were controlled for (Brück 2004b). Further, female-headed households, as well as ethnic minorities and households previously employed in the primary sector, were the displaced households in Colombia most vulnerable to low consumption (Ibáñez and Moya 2006).

Using household data from northern Uganda, and after controlling for other factors, Sarah Ssewanyana, Stephen Younger, and Ibrahim Kasirye (2007) find that female- and widow-headed households were not significantly worse off than male-headed households. Aside from systematic geographical differences in people's well-being caused by the high concentration of rebel attacks and crime in certain subregions, household consumption was particularly dependent on the household head's educational attainment—a measure that is, in turn, often heavily influenced by gender.

When women living in the household of their husbands are considered, the evaluation of their post-conflict welfare should also take into account the intrahousehold allocation of resources. Unequal bargaining power between men and women may have particularly dramatic consequences for child and female nutrition and morbidity in post-conflict periods, when resources are scarce. Economic destitution may also lead to the return of a single mother into her parents' household to share costs and income (De Herdt 2007). In general, intrahousehold dynamics are important to look at when evaluating individual welfare from a gender perspective—though the collection of appropriate data proves to be very difficult.

Health

The direct health effects on individuals involved in conflict may include death or injury and severe psychological problems (Guha-Sapir and Panhuis 2004). In addition, violent conflict is associated with various indirect health impacts. Wars frequently lead to the deterioration of public health, caused by the destruction of health facilities and infrastructure, the loss of skilled medical personnel, and reductions in government health spending (Iqbal 2006).

Life expectancy at birth is on average only marginally lower in conflict-affected developing countries than in countries at peace, with negligible gender differences (see table 1, panel C). The regional decomposition, however, reveals that in Africa, average life expectancies are significantly lower in war-torn societies (see table 2, panel C). A lack of access to maternity care and decreased food security (as indicated by a higher average prevalence of undernourishment in wartime and postwar periods, especially in Africa; see tables 1 and 2, panel C) are likely to result in increased infant and maternal mortality rates. Thomas Grein et al. (2003) find significantly higher child mortality rates among displaced households in post-conflict Angola, where malnutrition is a major cause of death. Malnourishment was also found among the children of displaced households in Colombia (Ibáñez and Moya 2006).

But Kavita Singh et al. (2005) find no significantly higher under-five mortality rates for long-term displaced populations when comparing them to the host population in northwestern Uganda and southern Sudan. Their analysis indicates no significant sex differentials in child mortality, nor did the sex of the household head influence mortality rates significantly. M. Hynes et al. (2002) present similar results in their comparative analysis of health outcomes in 52 refugee camps in seven countries, finding that the displaced persons had better reproductive health than the populations both in the host countries and in the countries of origin. Better access to health care services and to food and nonfood items in refugee camps, as well as the improved water supply and sanitation, is an obvious explanation.

In general, water-related and vector-borne infectious diseases may spread because immunization coverage declines and exposure to polluted water increases. In fact, immunization coverage against measles is found to be, on average, significantly lower in war-affected areas (see table 1, panel C), particularly (but not only) in African countries (see table 2, panel C). Relatively high immunization rates in post-conflict times might reflect the positive impact of international assistance.

Further, the risk of infection by HIV and other sexually transmitted diseases greatly increases during and in the wake of conflict. Observed higher average fertility rates in conflict times (see table 1, panel C) might also result from rising levels of mobility and a high prevalence of sexual violence and prostitution. Women and girls thus seem particularly vulnerable when they are forced to flee their homes (WHO 2002). Philip Verwimp and Jan Van Bavel (2005) show that although Rwandan refugees had higher fertility, the survival chances for their offspring—especially their daughters—were significantly lower than for the offspring of non-refugees. Moreover, mortality was significantly higher among the children of widowed, divorced, or single women.

The health impacts of armed conflict thus last far beyond the end of war. Richard Akresh, Philip Verwimp, and Tom Bundervoet (2007) analyze the effects of civil conflict in Rwanda on children's health status several years later and find that the height of children is significantly lower in those regions affected by civil war. Again, girls and children of unmarried mothers are much more susceptible to poor health outcomes. Using longitudinal data from rural Zimbabwe, Harold Alderman, John Hoddinott, and Bill Kinsey (2006) first show the negative impact of civil war on early childhood nutrition, and second prove the positive long-term relationship between preschoolers' nutritional status and both their height and their educational attainment in adolescence. Using cross-national data on disability-adjusted life years lost to various diseases and conditions, Hazem Adam Ghobarah, Paul Huth, and Bruce Russett (2003) find that the risks of death and disability from many infectious diseases rise sharply in war-affected countries, and that women and children are the most common long-term victims.

In sum, prevailing insecurity and violence are likely to remain a constant threat to women's health, as well as to their often precarious nutrition and access to food. The time and expense required to reconstruct destroyed health facilities and a general failure to invest resources in public health care in post-conflict situations often limit access to medical treatment, most notably in rural areas. The population groups most vulnerable to economic destitution—particularly women and children, as well as refugees and displaced people—are the most affected by the postwar breakdown of health and social services.

Education

Schooling is likely to be reduced or even completely stopped during violent conflict. The summary statistics for the developing world reveal that government spending on education as well as enrollment rates in secondary education are, on average, significantly lower in conflict-affected countries than in countries at peace (see table 1, panel D).

A growing number of studies have examined these effects of violent conflict on access to schooling at the micro level. During conflict, decreasing enrollment has been observed for Rwanda (Lopez and Wodon 2005), Uganda (Deininger 2003), and Tajikistan (Shemyakina 2006). David Evans and Edward Miguel (2005) find for rural Kenya that a parent's death, and particularly the loss of the mother, significantly increased the risk that young children would drop out of school. But Frances Stewart, Cindy Huang, and Michael Wang (2001) find decreasing enrollment in primary school in only three out of eighteen African countries, while in five countries rates even increased during civil conflicts.

When it comes to the post-conflict resumption of schooling, enrollment rates seem to recover relatively soon after the end of war, as shown for Rwanda (Lopez and Wodon 2005), Vietnam (Miguel and Roland 2006), Indonesia (Thomas et al. 2004), and Tajikistan (Shemyakina 2006). Still, depending on the war's length, the interruption of schooling often has severe, long-lasting consequences for the children's future employment opportunities and for the household's stock of human capital.

The conflict-related disruption of schooling seems to affect girls, on average, somewhat more than boys, as suggested by a decreasing ratio of girls to boys in primary and secondary education and by larger average decreases in female secondary enrollment rates (see table 1, panel D). Olga Shemyakina (2006) provides an in-depth analysis of the impacts of the civil war in Tajikistan: during conflict, the enrollment rates of young adults (ages 15–18 years) declined by more than 30 percentage points. Adolescent girls—especially those living in areas of high-intensity conflict—were most likely to be pulled out of school and had a lower probability of completing mandatory schooling.

Similar results are obtained by Ibáñcz and Moya (2006) in their analysis of displaced people in Colombia: here, the school attendance for children in primary school was even higher than it was in their hometown (due to more comprehensive educational services in the destination communities), but significantly lower for those in secondary education, who often had to contribute to income-generating activities. Children of households headed by females were thus more likely to drop out of school, while the household's participation in state-run programs to generate income had no significant effect on the school attendance of boys or girls.

However, Stewart, Huang, and Wang's (2001) study on conflict on the African continent finds that boys were more likely to drop out of school than girls because they are more likely to serve in the army. Given these sometimes contradictory results, the gendered impact of armed conflict on schooling remains unclear, varying with context. Still, girls in secondary education seem to be particularly vulnerable to the interruption of school attendance during conflict.

In general, and depending on the war's length, the interruption of schooling often has severe long-lasting consequences for the children's future employment opportunities and the household's stock of human capital. Efforts to maintain schooling during conflict, as undertaken in some cases by women's grassroots organizations in refugee camps (Sørensen 1998), and to resume schooling early in the aftermath of war should, therefore, be high on the agenda of post-conflict reconstruction. But in some cases, the losers' access to education has been restricted, as their enrollment has been limited or schools have been segregated along racial, ethnic, or religious lines (Justino 2006). Moreover, prewar gender disparities in the access to education often continue in the post-conflict period: the resumed schooling often builds on the prewar system, and girls continue to be left out for economic, cultural, or security reasons.

Conclusions

This chapter has examined the specific economic situations that women face in post-conflict settings. Analyzing both the theoretically expected and the empirically observed effects of war on the economic situation of women, we identify how violent conflict shapes constraints on women, determines their choices, and drives their socioeconomic outcomes. The analysis yields the following insights.

Constraints. The postwar economic circumstances of women are largely shaped by prewar societal norms on the one hand and the causes, objectives, conduct, and legacies of war on the other. This realization is key to understanding postwar gender relations, especially as war itself is a highly gendered process. Important gendered war legacies are played out in a very domestic sphere. The decision-making processes within a household and its distribution of resources are affected by war, while the forms of gender discrimination and abuse practiced within families and households are likely to rise and are unlikely to be reduced quickly in the postwar period. In fact, for women the negative legacies of war are likely to persist for a particularly long time, given their partly domestic character.

Furthermore, these harmful effects may be very hard to either measure or to fight with the standard policy instruments of reconstruction. The possible economic and social gains of women resulting from shifts in gender relations during war are therefore often at risk in the post-conflict period, when the affected societies—which are mostly male-dominated—tend to again allocate roles in traditional ways and to coerce women to resume their prewar domestic roles. The analysis has also clearly identified several groups of women and girls who are at risk of suffering significant discrimination and exploitation, as well as being overlooked in development efforts. These include displaced women, women employed in the informal sector, women in isolated areas, female ex-combatants, and girls and women in female-headed households.

Choices. Outside of the home, a key issue is women's participation in the labor market in the post-conflict period, as they engage in formal and informal employment. If violent conflict reduces the chances of women to join the labor force, especially in the formal sector, then this loss of opportunity creates a significant barrier to gender equality. Compounding the problem are institutional obstacles to equal economic opportunity, most notably legislation on rights to land and other property that has a strong gender bias, which curtails women's involvement in some forms of agriculture and in credit markets.

Outcomes. Overall, the effect of war on women's long-term social and economic position is ambiguous. In some instances, war may induce changes in gender roles, if only by imposing on society new modes of production or decision making, which are not entirely reversible in the postwar period. Some types of war may freeze existing formal and informal institutions in place, thereby reducing the rate of social change and institution building. In other instances, the conduct of war may shift gender relations by applying pressure to existing social norms. In other words, the primacy of war may displace competing discourses, including those on changing gender relations. In many if not most cases, however, war will have a plainly negative effect on women, who must cope with the general rise in violence and crime, the continuing limits imposed by male-dominated social norms, and the widespread breakdown of social services and infrastructure. This is likely to persist in the postwar period, thereby shaping gender

relations even in the so-called period of peace—a point that again under-
scores that the negative impact of war on women will probably be very
persistent.

Actors involved in planning and implementing post-conflict reconstruction efforts need to be aware of the different roles and needs of men and
women. As the burden of rebuilding a society after conflict also constitutes
a unique opportunity for reforming traditional institutions and removing
prewar gender disparities, post-conflict reconstruction efforts should take
advantage of possible changes in gender roles to tackle women's low level of
representation in political participation generally and, more specifically, in
formal peacebuilding processes. Equal access to resources, education, training, and employment are further prerequisites to women's economic empowerment in post-conflict societies.

References

Abirafeh, L. 2007. "Freedom Is Only Won from the Inside: Domestic Violence in Post-
Conflict Afghanistan." In *Change from Within: Diverse Perspectives on Domestic Vio-
lence in Muslim Communities,* ed. M. B. Alkhateeb and S. E. Abugideiri, 117–31.
Great Falls, VA: Peaceful Families Project.
Addison, T., and T. Brück. eds. 2009. *Making Peace Work: The Challenges of Social and
Economic Reconstruction.* Basingstoke: Palgrave Macmillan.
Akresh, R., P. Verwimp, and T. Bundervoet. 2007. "Civil War, Crop Failure, and Child
Stunting in Rwanda." World Bank Policy Research Working Paper 4208. World
Bank, Washington, DC.
Alderman, H., J. Hoddinott, and B. Kinsey. 2006. "Long Term Consequences of Early
Childhood Malnutrition." *Oxford Economic Papers* 58:450–74.
Berdal, M., and D. M. Malone, eds. 2000. *Greed and Grievance: Economic Agendas in
Civil Wars.* Boulder, CO: Lynne Rienner Publishers.
Bop, C. 2001. "Women in Conflicts, Their Gains and Their Losses." In *The Aftermath:
Women in Post-Conflict Transformation,* ed. S. Meintjes, M. Thursen, and A. Pillay,
19–34. London: Zed Books.
Bouta, T., G. Frerks, and I. Bannon. 2005. *Gender, Conflict, and Development.* Washing-
ton, DC: World Bank.
Brück, T. 2004a. "Coping Strategies in Post-War Rural Mozambique." HiCN Working
Paper 02. University of Sussex, Falmer-Brighton.
Brück, T. 2004b. "The Welfare Effects of Farm Household Activity Choices in Post-War
Mozambique." HiCN Working Paper 04. University of Sussex, Falmer-Brighton.
Brück, T., and K. Schindler. 2009a. "The Impact of Violent Conflicts on Households:
What Do We Know and What Should We Know about War Widows?" *Oxford De-
velopment Studies* 37:289–309.
Brück, T., and K. Schindler. 2009b. "Smallholder Land Access in Post-War Northern
Mozambique." *World Development* 37:1379–89.
Brück, T., and K. Van den Broeck. 2006. "Growth, Employment and Poverty in Mozam-
bique." Issues in Employment and Poverty Discussion Paper 21. International Labour
Organisation, Geneva.

Bundervoet, T. 2006. "Estimating Poverty in Burundi." HiCN Working Paper 20. University of Sussex, Falmer-Brighton.

Bundervoet, T. 2007. "Livestock, Crop Choice and Conflict: Evidence from Burundi." HiCN Working Paper 24. University of Sussex, Falmer-Brighton.

Chalmers, M. 2007. "Spending to Save? The Cost-Effectiveness of Conflict Prevention." *Defence and Peace Economics* 18:1–23.

Chen, M., J. Vanek, F. Lund, J. Heintz with R. Jhabvala, and C. Bonner. 2005. *Progress of the World's Women 2005: Women, Work and Poverty*. New York: United Nations Development Fund for Women.

Chingono, M. 1996. "War, Economic Crisis and the Emergence of the Grassroots War Economy." Chapter 3 in *The State, Violence and Development: The Political Economy of War in Mozambique, 1975–1992*, 71–126. Aldershot: Avebury.

Collier, P., and A. Hoeffler. 2004. "Conflicts." In *Global Crises, Global Solutions*, ed. B. Lomborg, 129–56. Cambridge: Cambridge University Press.

Couldrey, M., and T. Morris, eds. 2007. *Sexual Violence: Weapon of War, Impediment to Peace*. Forced Migration Review 27. Oxford: Refugee Studies Centre.

De Herdt, T. 2007. "Hiding from Regress: Poverty and Changing Household Composition in Congo-Kinshasa." Paper presented at the Second Annual Workshop, Households in Conflict Network, Antwerp, 19–20 January 2007.

De Watteville, N. 2002. "Addressing Gender Issues in Demobilization and Reintegration Programmes." World Bank Africa Region Working Paper Series 33. World Bank, Washington, DC.

Deininger, K. 2003. "Causes and Consequences of Civil Strife: Micro-Level Evidence from Uganda." *Oxford Economic Papers* 55:579–606.

Evans, D. K., and E. Miguel. 2005. "Orphans and Schooling in Africa: A Longitudinal Analysis." Center for International and Development Economics Research, Working Paper C05-143. Department of Economics, University of California, Berkeley.

Fearon, J., and D. Laitin. 2001. "Ethnicity, Insurgency and Civil War." *American Political Science Review* 97:75–90.

Fox, M. 2004. "Girl Soldiers: Human Security and Gendered Insecurity." *Security Dialogue* 35:465–79.

Ghobarah, H. A., P. Huth, and B. Russett. 2003. "Civil Wars Kill and Maim People— Long After the Shooting Stops." *American Political Science Review* 97:189–202.

Gleditsch, N. P., P. Wallensteen, M. Eriksson, M. Sollenberg, and H. Strand. 2002. "Armed Conflict 1946–2001: A New Dataset." *Journal of Peace Research* 39:615–37.

Greenberg, M., D. McMillan, B. Neto do Espirito Santo, and J. Ornelas. 1997. *Women's Participation in Angola's Reconstruction and in Its Political Institutions and Processes*. A Women in Development Technical Assistance Project. 2 vols. Washington, DC: WIDTECH.

Grein, T., F. Checchi, M. Escriba, A. Tamrat, U. Karunakara, C. Stokes, V. Brown, and D. Legros. 2003. "Mortality among Displaced Former UNITA Members and Their Families in Angola: A Retrospective Cluster Survey." *British Medical Journal* 327:650.

Guha-Sapir, D., and W. G. Panhuis. 2004. "Conflict-related Mortality: An Analysis of 37 Datasets." *Disasters* 28:418–28.

Handrahan, L. 2004. "Conflict, Gender, Ethnicity and Post-Conflict Reconstruction." *Security Dialogue* 35:429–45.

Hynes, M., M. Sheik, H. Wilson, and H. Spiegel. 2002. "Reproductive Health Indicators and Outcomes among Refugees and Internally Displaced Persons in Post-emergency Phase Camps." *Journal of the American Medical Association* 288:595–603.

Ibáñez, A. M., and A. Moya. 2006. "The Impact of Intra-State Conflict on Economic Welfare and Consumption Smoothing: Empirical Evidence for the Displaced Population in Colombia." HiCN Working Paper 23. University of Sussex, Falmer-Brighton.

Internal Displacement Monitoring Centre (IDMC). 2006. *Internal Displacement, Global Overview of Trends and Developments in 2005*. Geneva: Internal Displacement Monitoring Centre, Norwegian Refugee Council.

Inter-Parliamentary Union. 2009. *Women in Parliament in 2008: The Year in Perspective.* Geneva: Inter-Parliamentary Union.

Iqbal, Z. 2006. "Health and Human Security: The Public Health Impact of Violent Conflict." *International Studies Quarterly* 50:631–49.

Jaji, R. 2009. "Masculinity on Unstable Ground: Young Refugee Men in Nairobi, Kenya." *Journal of Refugee Studies* 22:177–94.

Justino, P. 2006. "On the Links between Violent Conflict and Chronic Poverty: How Much Do We Really Know?" HiCN Working Paper 18. University of Sussex, Falmer-Brighton.

Justino, P., and P. Verwimp. 2006. "Poverty Dynamics, Violent Conflict and Convergence in Rwanda." HiCN Working Paper 16. University of Sussex, Falmer-Brighton.

Jütting, J. P., C. Morrisson, J. Dayton-Johnson, and D. Drechsler. 2006. "Measuring Gender (In)Equality: Introducing the Gender, Institutions and Development Data Base (GID)." OECD Development Center, Working Paper 247. DEV/DOC(2006)01. OECD, Paris.

Klasen, S. 2002. "Low Schooling for Girls, Slower Growth for All? Cross-Country Evidence on the Effect of Gender Inequality in Education on Economic Development." *World Bank Economic Review* 16:345–73.

Kondylis, F. 2010. "Conflict Displacement and Labor Market Outcomes in Post-war Bosnia and Herzegovina." *Journal of Development Economics* 93:235–42.

Kumar, K. 2001. "Aftermath: Women and Women's Organizations in Postconflict Societies: The Role of International Assistance." USAID Program and Operations Assessment Report No. 28. Available at http://pdf.usaid.gov/pdf_docs/PNACG621.pdf (accessed 18 August 2010).

Lacina, B., and N. P. Gleditsch. 2005. "Monitoring Trends in Global Combat: A New Dataset of Battle Deaths." *European Journal of Population* 21:145–66.

Li, Q., and M. Wen. 2005. "The Immediate and Lingering Effects of Armed Conflict on Adult Mortality: A Time-Series Cross-National Analysis." *Journal of Peace Research* 42:471–92.

Lopez, J. H., and Q. Wodon. 2005. "The Economic Impact of Armed Conflict in Rwanda." *Journal of African Economies* 14:586–602.

Martin, S. 2005. *Must Boys Be Boys? Ending Sexual Exploitation and Abuse in UN Peacekeeping Missions.* Washington, DC: Refugees International.

McKay, A., and S. Loveridge. 2005. "Exploring the Paradox of Rwandan Agricultural Household Income and Nutritional Outcomes in 1990 and 2000." Staff Paper 2005-06, Department of Agricultural Economics, Michigan State University.

Meintjes, S. 2001. "War and Post-War Shifts in Gender Relations." In *The Aftermath: Women in Post-Conflict Transformation*, ed. S. Meintjes, M. Thursen, and A. Pillay, 63–77. London: Zed Books.

Miguel, E., and G. Roland. 2006. "The Long Run Impact of Bombing Vietnam." National Bureau of Economic Research Working Paper Series 11954, Cambridge, MA.

Moser, A. 2007. "Gender and Indicators, Overview Report." BRIDGE Publication, Institute of Development Studies, University of Sussex, Brighton.

Neild, R. 2001. "Democratic Police Reforms in War-torn Societies." *Conflict, Security and Development* 1:21–43.

Preston, R. 1994. "Returning Exiles in Namibia since Independence." In *When Refugees Go Home: African Experiences*, ed. T. Allen and H. Morsink, 260–67. Geneva: UNRISD; London: James Currey; Trenton, NJ: Africa World Press.

Rubio-Marín, R., ed. 2006. *What Happened to the Women? Gender and Reparations for Human Rights Violations.* New York: Social Science Research Council.

Shemyakina, O. 2006. "The Effect of Armed Conflict on Accumulation of Schooling: Results from Tajikistan." HiCN Working Paper 12. University of Sussex, Falmer-Brighton.

Singh, K., U. Karunakara, G. Burnham, and K. Hill. 2005. "Forced Migration and Under-Five Mortality: A Comparison of Refugees and Hosts in North-Western Uganda and Southern Sudan." *European Journal of Population* 21:247–70.

Sivard, R. L. 1996. *World Military and Social Expenditures 1996.* Washington, DC: World Priorities.

Small Arms Survey. 2005. *Small Arms Survey 2005.* Oxford: Oxford University Press.

Sørensen, B. 1998. "Women and Post-Conflict Reconstruction: Issues and Sources." WSP Occasional Paper 3. UN Research Institute for Social Development, Geneva.

Ssewanyana, S., S. Younger, and I. Kasirye. 2007. "Poverty under Conflict: The Case for Northern Uganda." Paper presented at the Center for the Study of African Economies Conference 2007, "Economic Development in Africa," Oxford, 18–20 March 2007.

Stewart, F., and V. FitzGerald, eds. 2001. *War and Underdevelopment.* 2 vols. Oxford: Oxford University Press.

Stewart, F., C. Huang, and M. Wang. 2001. "Internal Wars: An Empirical Overview of the Economic and Social Consequences." In *War and Underdevelopment*, ed. F. Stewart and V. FitzGerald, vol. 1, *The Economic and Social Consequences of Conflict*, 67–103. Oxford: Oxford University Press.

Strickland, R., and N. Duvvury. 2003. *Gender Equity and Peacebuilding: From Rhetoric to Reality: Finding the Way.* Washington, DC: International Center for Research on Women.

Thomas, D., K. Beegle, E. Frankenberg, B. Sikoki, J. Strauss, and G. Teruel. 2004. "Education in a Crisis." *Journal of Development Economics* 74:53–85.

United Nations. 2006. *The Millennium Development Goals Report 2006.* New York: United Nations.

United Nations Development Programme (UNDP). 2003. *Gender Approaches in Conflict and Post Conflict Situations.* New York: Bureau for Crisis Prevention and Recovery, UNDP.

UN Office for the Coordination of Humanitarian Affairs (OCHA) / Integrated Regional Information Networks (IRIN). 2007. *The Shame of War: Sexual Violence against Women and Girls in Conflict.* New York: IRIN.

United Nations Transitional Administration in East Timor (UNTAET). 2002. "Gender Equality Promotion." April. Fact Sheet 11, Office of Communication and Public Information.

U.S. Committee for Refugees and Immigrants (USCRI). 2006. *World Refugee Survey 2006.* Available at www.refugees.org/article.aspx?id=1565&subm=19&ssm=29&area=Investigate (accessed 2 July 2010).

Verpoorten, M. 2009. "Household Coping in War- and Peacetime: Cattle Sales in Rwanda, 1991–2001." *Journal of Development Economics* 88:67–86.

Verpoorten, M., and L. Berlage. 2007. "Economic Mobility in Rural Rwanda: A Study of the Effects of War and Genocide at the Household Level." *Journal of African Economies* 16:349–92.

Verwimp, P., and J. Van Bavel. 2005. "Child Survival and Fertility of Refugees in Rwanda." *European Journal of Population* 21:271–90.

Watson, C. 1996. *The Flight, Exile and Return of Chadian Refugees: A Case Study with a Special Focus on Women.* Geneva: UNRISD.

World Health Organization (WHO). 2002. *World Report on Violence and Health.* Ed. E. G. Krug et al. Geneva: World Health Organization.

6

Women and War

An Agenda for Action

Donald Steinberg

For advocates of the empowerment and protection of women in conflict situations, these are heady times. The past two years have seen a growing international awareness not only of the personal costs women pay for our failure to protect them in the context of armed conflict but also of the tremendous collective costs we pay as a global community for failing to achieve our goals of building peace, pursuing development, and reconstructing post-conflict societies. The result of this awareness has been a spate of UN Security Council resolutions, national action plans, impressive speeches, and structural changes that have, we hope, set the stage for real progress.

It is tragic that it has taken graphic images of women raped in the eastern Congo, and young girls who had acid thrown in their faces in Afghanistan for daring to return to school, to shame our collective conscience, but the world is responding. At the United Nations, UN Action against Sexual Violence in Conflict has been formed to coordinate enhanced work by thirteen separate agencies under the tagline "Stop Rape Now."[1] UN Security Council resolutions—1820 (2008), 1888 (2009), and 1889 (2009) in

---

1. The thirteen entities are the Department of Political Affairs, Department of Peacekeeping Operations, Office for the Coordination of Humanitarian Affairs, Office of the High Commissioner for Human Rights, Peacebuilding Support Office, Joint Program on HIV/AIDS, UN Development Program, UN Population Fund, High Commissioner for Refugees, UN Children's Fund, UN Development Fund for Women, World Food Program, and World Health Organization.

particular—have created an office of a special representative for eliminating violence against women, mandated new measures of accountability, called for structures to name and shame offending parties, authorized the use of UN sanctions in such cases, and defined widespread sexual violence itself as a threat to international peace and security.

No Security Council peacekeeping mandate can be passed now without a paragraph requiring forceful civilian protection, especially for women. The creation of a new UN gender entity—UN Women—has the potential to end the disarray that has bedeviled the efforts of the UN Development Fund for Women, the Office of the Special Advisor for Gender Issues, the Division for the Advancement of Women, and their sister agencies, if key steps are taken to ensure its effectiveness and relevance. The same promise and caveats apply to the High-Level Steering Committee for Women, Peace and Security, which is chaired by Deputy Secretary-General Asha Rose Migiro and backed by a civil society advisory group led by former Irish president Mary Robinson and the head of the Femmes Africa Solidarité, Bineta Diop.

Other international and regional organizations—notably the European Union, the African Union, and the Organization for Security and Cooperation in Europe—are taking similar steps. The European Union has adopted a "comprehensive approach" for implementing Resolutions 1325 and 1820, which includes provisions for building political will, training political and military officials, exchanging information on best practices, cooperating with international actors, monitoring, and evaluating (Council of the European Union 2008). The European Union is also articulating an action plan on gender equality and women's empowerment, complementing national action plans adopted by nine EU member-states. In the first half of 2010, the Spanish presidency made gender considerations in the context of armed conflict prevention one of its top priorities, as has the Belgian presidency as of July 2010. The European Union has reached out to civil society groups, including the European Peacebuilding Liaison Office, with which it is developing indicators for it to use in analyzing and demanding accountability for such considerations.

The Nordic countries have long shown the way in this agenda, but now they are being joined by other governments. In the United States, a fortified and reenergized office for global women's affairs was established at the State Department under Melanne Verveer. New programs within the U.S. Agency for International Development and the State Department's Bureau of Population, Refugees, and Migration, as well as the leadership of President Barack Obama, Secretary of State Hillary Clinton, and UN Ambassador Susan Rice, are encouraging. Secretary Clinton highlighted the tragedy of sexual violence during her first visit to Africa, reaffirming the centrality of gender issues to the global achievement of U.S. foreign policy objectives. In Congress, Senator John Kerry, the chairman of the Senate Foreign Relations Committee, and Congressman Bill Delahunt have sponsored and gained new support for the International Violence Against Women Act, legislation that outlines comprehensive measures to strengthen U.S. and UN initiatives on these issues. A former sponsor, Vice President Joseph Biden, is in a new position to push for its enactment.

But against this backdrop, two "inconvenient" questions bedevil us. First, has this effort had any tangible effect on the ground? Substantive and anecdotal evidence suggests that we are making little progress against sexual abuse, impunity, and the systematic disengagement of women in conflict situations. Rape continues to be used unabated as a weapon of war. The voices of women are still excluded from peace tables, resulting in agreements that ill reflect ground truth and are as likely to fail to bring lasting peace as to succeed. Issues related to trafficking in persons, reproductive health care, girls' education, and accountability for past abuses continue to be lost in the shuffle. Warring parties still frequently begin peace processes by granting amnesties to each other for heinous crimes committed in the fighting—tantamount to men with guns forgiving other men with guns for atrocities carried out against women.

A second nagging doubt is whether the expression of political will by senior policymakers has been translated into a higher priority for gender considerations when national security policies are adopted. Regrettably, strategic decisions are still generally made with little if any regard for their impact on women. In the eastern Congo, for example, regional powers were backed by the world's superpowers and even the United Nations in attacks in 2009 against the Democratic Forces for the Liberation of Rwanda and the Lord's Resistance Army. These are indeed horrendous groups, but the attacks produced few if any strategic gains against them and were structured so as to virtually invite massive retaliation against the local population. The predictable results were targeted rapes against women and massive displacement of hundreds of thousands of women-led households. And it was not just the retaliation of renegade forces that violated international humanitarian law: the very Congolese and Ugandan forces who led the attacks are themselves charged with brutal human rights abuses against women. Similarly, in Afghanistan we still hear domestic and even international policymakers argue that long-term security and counterinsurgency efforts depend on winning the support of warlords, traditional leaders, and even Taliban figures, whom we cannot afford to alienate through an overemphasis on women's rights and protection.

Thus, we face real challenges in how to translate our growing awareness and activism into concrete improvements on the ground, both by prioritizing these issues in the corridors of power and by ensuring the adoption and implementation of effective programs and projects with rapid impact.

The Promise of UNSCR 1325

To design an action agenda for UNSCR 1325, it is important to view the resolution in its proper historical context. Based on the Namibia Plan of Action on Mainstreaming a Gender Perspective in Multidimensional Peace Support Operations (adopted in Windhoek in May 2000), the resolution's eighteen articles called for greater representation of women in national decision making, especially in the prevention and resolution of conflict; incorporation of a gender perspective into peacekeeping operations; new financial and logistical support for gender dimensions of peace-building and post-conflict reconstruction; greater consideration of women and girls in resettlement, rehabilitation, and demobilization programs; respect for women's human rights and an end to impunity for crimes against women; new efforts to combat sexual violence in armed conflict; and greater consultations with local and international women's groups.

But Resolution 1325 was a product of its times. It reflected a clear cautiousness among the Security Council members in 2000 about wading into thematic issues and a lack of confidence in declaring that these issues themselves constituted a threat to international peace and security. Thus, its language is hortatory rather than directive: it "urges," "encourages," "requests," and "invites" rather than "demands" or "instructs." The resolution lacks time-bound targets for achieving its goals, accountability or measurement provisions to secure its implementation, working groups or special representatives to monitor and prod action, new funding or personnel dedicated to the issue, reporting mechanisms vis-à-vis the Security Council, watch lists of countries failing to meet its objectives as a naming and shaming exercise, or provisions for sanctions against state and nonstate violators. Contrast this approach with that of UNSCR 1612 on children and armed conflict, which was passed five years later and included each of these provisions.

Some observers believe that these deficiencies doomed Resolution 1325 from the outset. This is unfair. As documented elsewhere in this volume, there has been notable progress within UN structures, especially in terms of awareness, expansion of the numbers and roles of gender advisers, gender training for peacekeepers and senior officials, adoption of some outstanding guidelines for field action, development of small-scale and in situ programs, and more. But the tenth anniversary of the resolution reminds us that for women in conflict, its promise is still largely a dream deferred. There is a growing realization that October 2010 must be not a celebration, nor even a stocktaking exercise, but an impetus for urgent new action to address the most serious problems. Concrete steps, elaborated below, must be taken to bring women to the peace table, expand assistance for gender-related post-conflict reconstruction, empower the newly established UN women's entity, strengthen women's associations in conflict-affected countries, mandate time-bound goals and accountability mechanisms for implementing the resolution, protect displaced women from sexual abuse, engage women in security sectors, and use moral suasion to force member-states to make formal commitments to specific actions over the next three years that will promote the resolution's provisions.

Where We Are and Where We Need to Go

In preparing for the second decade of action under Resolution 1325, UN officials have recognized that the United Nations can accomplish little unless it partners with member-states and activists from around the world who can bring their expertise, experience, and especially ground truth to this exercise. One key step has been the establishment in March 2010 of the UN Civil Society Advisory Group on Women, Peace and Security, to which have been appointed fourteen independent experts to advise senior UN officials on ways to better protect women in conflict situations, and to ensure that women's voices are heard in peace processes and post-conflict reconstruction and governance structures.[2] Its mandate and methodology are instructive.

As a first step, the advisory group is assessing the status of implementation of Resolution 1325: what has worked well, what has worked at the local or grassroots level but has not been replicated elsewhere or brought to scale, and where we have simply failed to meet our commitments.

Second, the advisory group will establish realistic and achievable time-bound goals for the areas identified as needing improvement. For example, what percentage of women do we need sitting at peace tables by what year? What reduction in sexual violence around UN-run camps for refugees and internally displaced persons must we achieve and by when? What portion of funds contributed at post-conflict donor conferences must be

---

2. As of July 2010, the members of the panel are Mary Robinson (Ireland), co-chair; Bineta Diop (Senegal), co-chair; Sanam Anderlini (Iran/United Kingdom); Thelma Awori (Liberia/Uganda); Sharon Bhagwan-Rolls (Fiji); Lahkdar Brahimi (Algeria); Nyaradzayi Gumbonzvanda (Zimbabwe); Swanee Hunt (United States); Hina Jilani (Pakistan); Elisabeth Rehn (Finland); Zainab Salbi (Iraq/United States); Salim Ahmed Salim (Tanzania); Donald Steinberg (United States); and Susana Villarán de la Puente (Peru).

dedicated to gender-based projects, such as reproductive health care and girls' education? The advisory group is supporting UN efforts to devise indicators to measure these outcomes, provisions to identify the entities and individuals responsible for achieving them, and accountability mechanisms to put pressure behind their implementation.

Finally, the advisory group is addressing the principal constraints to progress by assessing the institutional changes needed within the United Nations, other international and regional organizations, and member-states to facilitate progress. It is also addressing the need for additional financial and personnel resources, including a quick-disbursing trust fund available to UN officials leading peacekeeping missions to help them respond rapidly in situations of impending sexual violence or other abuses. In addition, the advisory group is serving as a catalyst to bring the voices and ground truth of women affected by armed conflict to the attention of global decision makers.

A Cautionary Tale from Angola

Before turning to the specific measures that should constitute the action agenda for UNSCR 1325 for the next decade, it is instructive to review a practical example of the costs of failing to involve women in peace processes. In this regard, my experience in Angola provides a cautionary tale.

In 1994, while serving as President Clinton's special assistant for African affairs, I supported negotiations to end two decades of civil war in Angola that had killed a half million people and left four million homeless. When the Lusaka Protocol (1994) was signed, I was asked by a journalist how the agreement took into account the needs of war-affected women. "Not a single provision in the agreement discriminates against women," I said, a little too proudly. "The agreement is gender-neutral."

President Clinton then named me ambassador to Angola. It took me only a few weeks after my arrival in Luanda in June 1995 to realize that a peace agreement that calls itself "gender-neutral" is, by definition, discriminatory against women and likely to fail.

First, the agreement did not require the participation of women in the Joint Commission, the peace implementation body. As a result, at a typical meeting of the commission there were forty men and no women sitting around the table. This imbalance silenced women's voices and meant that issues such as sexual violence, human trafficking, abuses by government and rebel security forces, reproductive health care, and girls' education were given short shrift, if addressed at all.

The peace accord was based on thirteen separate amnesties that forgave the parties for atrocities committed during the conflict. One amnesty went so far as to forgive the parties for any action they might take in the coming months. Given the prominence of sexual abuse during the conflict, the amnesties introduced cynicism into the heart of our efforts to rebuild the justice and security sectors. In effect, it showed Angolan women, as well as other key civil society actors, that the peace process was intended for the benefit of the ex-combatants and not them.

Similarly, demobilization programs for ex-combatants depended on lists provided by the warring parties. As a rule, they defined a combatant as anyone who carried a gun in combat. Thousands of women who had been kidnapped or coerced into the armed forces and served as cooks, bearers, messengers, and even sex slaves (so-called bush wives) were largely excluded. Further, camps for demobilized soldiers and even for displaced persons were rarely constructed with women in mind, and as a result women risked rape or death each time they left the camp to collect firewood or used latrines in isolated and dimly lit settings.

Male ex-combatants received demobilization assistance, but were sent back without skills or education to communities that had learned to live without them during decades of conflict. As is predictable in such situations, the frustration of these men exploded into an epidemic of alcoholism, drug abuse, divorce, rape, and domestic violence. This was especially true for young boys, who had never learned how to interact on an equal basis with girls their own age. In effect, the end of civil war simply unleashed a new era of violence against women and girls.

Even such well-intentioned efforts as clearing major roads of land mines to allow four million displaced persons to return to their homes backfired against women. Road clearance sometimes preceded the demining of fields, wells, and forests, resulting in premature resettlement and return. As women in this environment went out to plant the fields, fetch water, and collect firewood, they suffered a new rash of injuries from land mines.

Over time, we recognized these problems and brought out gender advisers and human rights officers; launched programs in reproductive health care, girls' education, microenterprise, and support for women's nongovernmental organizations (NGOs); and involved women in planning and implementing all our programs. But by then, civil society—and particularly women—had come to view the peace process as serving only the interests of the warring parties. When the process faltered in 1998, largely because of the intransigence of the rebel leader Jonas Savimbi, there was little public pressure on the leaders to prevent a return to conflict, and war soon broke out again. Permanent peace came only after Savimbi was killed in February 2002.

A key lesson from this experience is that peace itself is not enough to protect and empower women. How we make peace determines whether the end of armed conflict means a safer world for women or simply ushers in a different and in some cases more pernicious era of violence against them. Sadly, we have not learned this lesson very well, as shown by developments in Afghanistan. Given the Taliban's abhorrent record on women's rights during its reign, it is stunning that the insurgents are scoring some debate points by arguing that women in Afghanistan today suffer more broadly from the lack of security, corruption, rights abuses, and civilian casualties (see International Crisis Group 2008). Indeed, advances in political participation by women and school attendance by girls have been offset by a failure to insist on accountability for warlords whose forces committed sexual violence during the years of conflict and continue such abuse today. Instead, a number of these criminals have been given positions of power.

The murder of women leaders and human rights defenders in Afghanistan and the failure of the government to identify and prosecute their assailants heighten the impression of a lack of national commitment to women's rights. Not only has the administration of Hamid Karzai failed to publicly articulate a vision of women's rights that is both homegrown and consistent with traditional Afghan Islamic society, but it has treated women's rights as a bargaining chip to win support from traditional leaders. Thus, it has ceded the debate to those who erroneously argue that such efforts reflect an alien concept imposed on Afghanistan by foreigners and their Afghan "puppets."

An Action Plan for Revitalizing UNSCR 1325

We can no longer afford to exclude the talents and insights of half the population in the pursuit of peace or to treat them as mere victims. Eight specific actions should be taken as a priority for the next decade.

First, those charged with leading and supporting peace processes, especially mediators from the United Nations and regional bodies, should commit to bring women to the table as peace negotiations are conducted and peace agreements are implemented. Around the world, talented women peacebuilders face discrimination in legal, cultural, and traditional practices, and threats of violence make even the most courageous women think twice before stepping forward. Groundbreaking research carried out under the direction of Anne-Marie Goetz, chief adviser for governance, peace, and security at the United Nations Development Fund for Women (UNIFEM), suggests that only one in thirteen participants in peace negotiations since 1992 has been a woman (UNIFEM 2009b).[3] Recent accords in Indonesia, Nepal, Somalia, Côte d'Ivoire, the Philip-

---

3. The research is ongoing, and data are updated as additional information is received.

pines, and the Central African Republic have not had a single woman signatory, mediator, or negotiator. Of 300 peace agreements negotiated since 1989, just 18 contain even a passing reference to sexual violence. Peace accords on Bosnia, Liberia, Sierra Leone, and Somalia—where such violence was a dominant feature of the fighting—are silent on this issue.

The usual rejoinder is that there simply are no women capable of participating in these processes, because of the male domination of security and conflict resolution issues. And yet in many of the affected regions, it is women who serve as the mediators of disputes at the community levels; in others, educated and successful women are active in sectors involving similar negotiations, including government, business, law, and academics (see International Crisis Group 2006). In northern Uganda, for example, women's associations such as the Teso Women's Peace Association, Kitgum Women's Peace Initiative, and Gulu District Women's Development Committee have played a key role in local dispute settlement and as peace activists, yet they were excluded from negotiations between the Ugandan government and the Lord's Resistance Army. In Sudan, the systematic exclusion of women from peace negotiations on Darfur in particular has contributed to the failure of all accords, including the May 2006 Darfur Peace Agreement, notwithstanding the existence of a vast pool of talented and educated Sudanese women—including graduates of the remarkable Afhad University for Women in Khartoum, where some 5,000 women are currently training.

The Security Council must insist that the mandate for every UN peacekeeping mission protect women peacebuilders by providing them personal security and promote their participation through training, financial stipends, and other means. The council should demand that negotiations led by the United Nations include a critical mass of qualified women—at least 25 percent—on all sides, even if doing so requires quotas (Krook 2009). Critics charged that such quotas are an aberration and represent reverse discrimination, but in fact they are now the norm around the world: for example, political parties and national legislatures in more than 100 countries have quotas for female candidates for elected office.

Second, bilateral contributors and multilateral institutions should insist that post-conflict recovery packages prioritize issues of importance to women, in particular reproductive health care and girls' education. In emergency funding projects to support twenty-three post-conflict situations between 2006 and 2009, only 3 percent included specific funding for women and girls (UNIFEM 2009a)[4]—this despite our knowledge that girls' education, for example, is one of the best investments that can be made to

---

4. Again, the research is ongoing, and data are updated as additional information is received.

promote stable societies, reduce unwanted pregnancies, improve agricultural methods, and eliminate sexual violence. It has been said: "Educate a boy and you help a person; educate a girl and you help a community."

Donors should also help women to attain economic independence through landownership, microenterprise, and skills training. All post-conflict recovery plans should be subjected to gender-impact analysis and should specify funds dedicated to women's needs. At the same time, gender considerations must be mainstreamed, so that the health minister will view reproductive health care as a top priority, the commerce minister will promote women's engagement in all levels of business activity, the education minister will stress girls' education from primary to tertiary levels, and so on. Women's issues are too important to be left to the women's ministry alone.

Third, the countries most instrumental in creating the new UN women's entity must ensure that it has the power, resources, and global reach to make a real difference. The creation of this office was a Faustian bargain: advocates abandoned their dream of a single agency with global reach and a billion dollars in dedicated funding, a so-called UNICEF for Women. In exchange, the General Assembly created a high-level office—UN Women—to oversee the significant but often competing contributions of UNIFEM, the Office of the Special Advisor for Gender Issues, the Division for the Advancement of Women, and other bodies, and to raise the profile of women's issues at the UN Secretariat in New York and in UN missions abroad. The European Union and United States in particular must extend generous voluntary contributions and the political support needed for the head of this office to be a forceful and ever-present advocate throughout the UN system and beyond. The new undersecretary-general must be a world-class figure, with the capacity to generate public attention, mobilize political will among governments, and work the UN system. Secretary-General Ban Ki-moon must give her—yes, it should be a woman—the respect and resources she needs to do her job, including direct access to the General Assembly and Security Council.[5]

Fourth, bilateral donors and multilateral institutions should expand assistance for private women's groups in conflict-affected countries. Civil society organizations are often the first victims of the polarization that accompanies internal armed conflicts. Women must have the institutional strength to influence local and global decisions that affect their lives. They should identify women's organizations as local partners in implementing projects: contracts for distributing humanitarian assistance, resolving disputes, and monitoring elections can provide even more support than

---

5. In September 2010, the former president of Chile, Michele Bachelet, was appointed head of UN Women.

programs directed specifically at strengthening institutions, especially if accompanied by mentoring programs. The principle must be "Nothing about us without us."

The training provided by the NGO "Pact" is instructive. Among its other programs, Pact organizes long-term training and mentoring for promising local nongovernmental organizations in the basics of management, grant proposal drafting, bookkeeping to international standards, and so on, and then supports these NGOs throughout their development process.[6] In 2009, Pact assisted more than 12,000 organizations in sixty-two countries, including through its groundbreaking WORTH program to empower women's businesses.

Fifth, the Security Council must demand that the United Nations adopt time-bound goals—backed by monitoring, accountability provisions, and enforcement mechanisms—for reducing violence against women, ensuring the participation of women in peace processes, providing reconstruction resources to projects of interest to women, and the like. The United Nations is currently engaging in a useful exercise to identify indicators in this regard in line with Resolution 1889, but the process must go further in mandating rewards for UN institutions and individuals for achieving these objectives and punishments for failing to do so. Further, to bring Resolution 1325 up to date, the Security Council should establish a permanent working group on sexual violence, issue a watch list of countries and nonstate actors of concern to be named and shamed into improving their records, require periodic reports by the secretary-general to the Security Council on these issues, and enshrine the principle that sanctions can be imposed on governments and nonstate actors that abuse or fail to protect women. Similar measures should be prioritized at regional organizations, including the African Union, the Organization of American States, and the Association of Southeast Asian Nations.

Sixth, the international humanitarian community should join together to protect one of the most vulnerable groups in conflict: those displaced from their homes and seeking refuge in camps for refugees and internally displaced persons (IDPs). A priority should be prevention of the rape of women and girls during the collection of fuel; an expansion of livelihood, health, and education programs; the mainstreaming of psychosocial considerations in all protection and services; training for camp managers and protection forces alike; proper configuration of camps; and engagement of women refugees and IDPs in decision making on these issues. Excellent guidelines are now in place from various UN bodies, including the High Commissioner for Refugees, on gender-based violence interventions in

---

6. More information about Pact is available at www.pactworld.org/cs/who_we_are/welcome.

these humanitarian settings (UNHCR 2003; Inter-Agency Standing Committee 2005, 2010). However, knowledge of these guidelines is incomplete and sometimes nonexistent among host governments, NGOs, displaced persons, peacekeeping forces, and even implementing UN agencies. Their systematic implementation is even sketchier, reflecting not only a lack of knowledge and familiarity with the guidelines but also inadequate financial and personnel resources, lack of high-level attention and prioritization, weak coordination, and the absence of goals and indicators needed to hold individuals and institutions accountable.[7]

The global body for official humanitarian agencies, the UN Inter-Agency Standing Committee, recently adopted guidance on addressing rape in the context of firewood collection, including the provision of cooking fuel in humanitarian settings, based on recommendations from the Women's Refugee Commission and other advocacy groups (see Women's Refugee Commission 2006; Inter-Agency Standing Committee 2009). The donor community should ensure funding to implement these provisions fully, starting with the high-risk regions of Sudan, Chad, eastern Congo, and the huge Dadaab refugee camp in Kenya.

Seventh, leading external supporters of security sector reform in post-conflict situations—the European Union, United States, and United Nations in particular—should ensure that their support to rebuild and reform armies, police, and other security forces includes effective training in gender issues for all personnel and requires ample incorporation of women into those forces. Bringing women into these forces is particularly important to ensure that women who have been abused will come forward with their accusations, as is establishing "family safety units" within police systems. Foreign troop contributors should also lead by example: the presence of all-female peacekeeping units—such as the Indian battalion in Liberia—is a welcome novelty, but it is far from enough. The European Union and United States should commit to providing teams of women military observers to peacekeeping mission and cease-fire monitoring teams. The North Atlantic Treaty Organization, the African Union, African subregional organizations, and other sources of peacekeeping forces should adopt similar programs.

Finally, there must be new financial resources dedicated to these efforts, provided through both assessed and voluntary contributions. There must be a quantum leap in the resources dedicated to these issues, espe-

---

7. One recent example of this failure is in the humanitarian response to the earthquake in Haiti. Despite clear IASC guidance regarding the design of sanitation efforts in humanitarian settings, as of April 2010, latrines were not divided between men and women in most IDP facilities, they did not have inside locks, and their lighting was insufficient. In these areas, a predictable and preventable pattern of rape and other sexual abuse resulted.

cially for projects in conflict-affected countries—$1 billion per year, or just about 30 cents per woman. An important initiative to mark the tenth anniversary of Resolution 1325 would be a global presidential- or ministerial-level pledging conference, where member-states would be under international pressure to come forward with formal commitments on concrete actions they will take over the next three years to promote the resolution's provisions. Partnerships should be encouraged, perhaps linking new resources from donor countries and new political will from conflicted-affected countries, on the model of the commitments made under the Clinton Global Initiative.[8]

How to Make It Happen: Lessons from Resolution 1820

What lessons can advocates of this agenda learn and adapt from the success in promoting action in international bodies over the past two years? Crucial lessons come from the efforts of like-minded advocates in civil society, the UN Secretariat, and key member-states during the first half of 2008 to pass a Security Council resolution on sexual violence in conflict. Growing recognition of the increasing use of rape as a weapon of war set the stage for action in early 2008, but advocates recognized that it was important to document and personalize the phenomenon. The importance of data from the ground on the patterns and prevalence of sexual violence in conflict cannot be overstressed. The most important use of such data is in developing projects and policies to prevent such violence and assist its victims,[9] but hard numbers also help create sufficient political will so that policymakers are prepared to dedicate scarce resources—including their own attention—to the problem. There are three critical elements: first, credible data to show that the problem is real and pressing; second, a convincing linkage between addressing the problem and achieving broader policy objectives; and third, a credible showing that a reasonable

---

8. The Clinton Global Initiative brings together international civil society actors, the business community, governments, foundations, and international organizations to make joint commitments to achieve time-bound goals in key social and economic sectors. Since its launch in 2005, the initiative has fostered 1,700 commitments generating some $57 billion in new resources.

9. Key insights can be derived from identifying the profile of perpetrators, for example. If most rapes are carried out by government security forces, then there is a clear need for expanded programs of security sector reform, more vigorous prosecution of individual soldiers/police and their commanders, expansion of the numbers of women in security forces, and new training in protection of civilians. A different kind of intervention is required if most rapes are perpetrated by rebel forces, family members, or unknown assailants. Similarly, if the data show high numbers of unreported rapes, steps should be taken to facilitate women's access to the justice system, to bring women into the police forces and expand community policing, to look at social mores that condone such behavior, and to conduct civic education programs to make individuals aware of their rights.

application of resources and attention can if not solve the problem then at least make a substantial improvement. Put simply: is the problem real, important, and solvable? Elsewhere, I have referred to the need to meet a "threshold of credibility" (Steinberg 2008).

The poster child of this effort was the tragic situation in eastern Congo. Personal accounts of sexual assaults were vital. Visits to foreign capitals by victims of rapes and those who treat them—including the courageous Dr. Denis Mukwege, who directs the Panzi Hospital in Bukavu, which treats rape victims from the region—had a major impact.[10] But it was important to go beyond testimonials and be able to say with full confidence that there were 27,000 reported cases of rape in the South Kivu province of eastern Congo, or some 70 rapes every day.

The fifteen ambassadors to the Security Council, all men, were lobbied by advocates, including their spouses. For example, they were made to watch films on sexual violence, such as the graphic *The Greatest Silence* (2007), directed by Lisa Jackson.[11] Efforts by UN Action against Sexual Violence in Conflict, including the hosting of a conference at Wilton Park outside London on peacekeepers' role in preventing sexual violence, helped personally invest key policymakers such as U.S. Ambassador Zalmay Khalilzad in this effort. Support from like-minded UN missions and Secretariat officials was essential. Pressure also came from U.S. Congressman Bill Delahunt, who headed the House of Representatives' oversight for the United Nations and held hearings on the effect of conflict on women in advance of the Security Council debate (U.S. Congress 2008).

The result was UNSCR 1820, passed in June 2008 under the U.S. presidency of the Council. The resolution breaks new ground by mandating wide-ranging and concrete actions by the UN Secretariat, member-states, and nonstate actors to combat sexual violence in conflict. Its passage is clear evidence of the wisdom of Margaret Mead's often-quoted statement: "Never doubt that a small group of thoughtful, committed citizens can change the world. Indeed, it is the only thing that ever has."[12]

But even in this success story, a cautionary note must be sounded. Members of the Security Council were by no means satisfied that they had a clear picture of the phenomenon. Resolution 1820 called for "analy-

---

10. Further information on the work of Denis Mukwege and the Panzi Hospital in Bukavu is available at www.panzihospitalbukavu.org/.

11. For more information on the film, upcoming screenings and events, and DVD purchase, see http://thegreatestsilence.org/.

12. The efforts of two talented and dedicated officers—Laurie Phipps and Phil Staltonstall at the U.S. and U.K. missions to the United Nations, respectively—cannot be overstated.

sis of prevalence and trends," "benchmarks for measuring progress," and plans for a lasting solution to the dearth of reliable data on sexual violence. It was as if the council was saying to the advocates: "We know this is a serious problem, but we do not know enough about what is going on or how to address it." This lack of information has delayed its implementation and even required that additional measures—UNSCRs 1888 and 1889—be adopted more than a year later to give the efforts real teeth.

The Road Ahead

We must move beyond words, resolutions, and stocktaking exercises to establish and implement an ambitious but achievable agenda for action on women and armed conflict. The success of our efforts will not be measured by the reports we issue, the resolutions and legislation we pass, the publicity we generate, or even the money we spend. It will be measured by the degree to which we protect the lives and well-being of women and girls faced with the horrors of war, empower them to play their rightful and vital role in peace processes and post-conflict reconstruction and governance, prevent armed thugs from abusing them in conditions of displacement, hold government security forces and warlords alike accountable for sexual abuses, prevent traffickers from turning women and girls into commodities, build strong civil society networks for women, and end the stigma of victimization that confronts women leaders.

This dream embodied in UNSCR 1325 must be deferred no longer. Langston Hughes (1995) reminds us of the risks of such deferral——does the dream "dry up," or "fester," or "just sag like a heavy load?" "Or does it explode?"

References

Council of the European Union. 2008. "Comprehensive Approach to the EU Implementation of the UN Security Council Resolutions 1325 and 1820 on Women, Peace and Security." 1 December. 15671/1/08. Available at www.consilium.europa.eu/ueDocs/cms_Data/docs/hr/news187.pdf (accessed 2 July 2010).

Hughes, L. 1995. "A Dream Deferred." In *The Collected Poems of Langston Hughes*, ed. A. Rampersad and D. Roessel, 426. New York: Vintage Classics.

Inter-Agency Standing Committee. 2005. *Guidelines for Gender-Based Violence Interventions in Humanitarian Settings: Focusing on Prevention of and Response to Sexual Violence in Emergencies*. September. Geneva: Inter-Agency Standing Committee. Available at www.unhcr.org/refworld/docid/439474c74.html (accessed 2 July 2010).

Inter-Agency Standing Committee. 2010. "Gender-Based Violence." Part IV.4 of *Handbook for the Protection of Internally Displaced Persons*, 167–89. June. Geneva: Inter-Agency Standing Committee. Available at www.unhcr.org/refworld/docid/4790cbc02.html (accessed 2 July 2010).

Inter-Agency Standing Committee Task Force on Safe Access to Firewood and Alternative Energy in Humanitarian Settings. 2009. *Matrix on Agency Roles and Responsibilities for Ensuring a Coordinated, Multi-Sectoral Fuel Strategy in Humanitarian Settings.* April. Geneva: Inter-Agency Standing Committee. Available at www.unhcr.org/refworld/pdfid/4ac5f1b22.pdf (accessed 2 July 2010).

International Crisis Group. 2006. "Beyond Victimhood: Women's Peacebuilding in Sudan, Congo and Uganda." Africa Report 112. 28 June. Available at www.crisisgroup.org/~/media/Files/africa/central-africa/Beyond%20Victimhood%20Womens%20Peacebuilding%20in%20Sudan%20Congo%20and%20Uganda.ashx (accessed 2 July 2010).

International Crisis Group. 2008. "Taliban Propaganda: Winning the War of Words?" Asia Report 158. 24 July. Available at www.crisisgroup.org/~/media/Files/asia/south-asia/afghanistan/158_taliban_propaganda___winning_the_war_of_words.ashx (accessed 2 July 2010).

Krook, M. L. 2009. *Quotas for Women in Politics: Gender and Candidate Selection Reform Worldwide.* New York: Oxford University Press.

Steinberg, D. 2008. "Combatting Sexual Violence in Conflict: Using Facts from the Ground." Speech delivered to UN Action against Sexual Violence in Conflict, 17 December, Geneva.

United Nations Development Fund for Women (UNIFEM). 2009a. "Funding for Women's Needs within Post-Conflict Needs Assessments (PCNAs)."

United Nations Development Fund for Women (UNIFEM). 2009b. "Women's Participation in Peace Negotiations: Connections between Presence and Influence." April. Available at www.realizingrights.org/pdf/UNIFEM_handout_Women_in_peace_processes_Brief_April_20_2009.pdf (accessed 2 July 2010).

United Nations High Commissioner for Refugees (UNHCR). 2003. *Sexual and Gender-Based Violence against Refugees, Returnees and Internally Displaced Persons: Guidelines for Prevention and Response.* May. Geneva: UNHCR. Available at www.unhcr.org/refworld/docid/3edcd0661.html (accessed 2 July 2010).

U.S. Congress. 2008. House Committee of Foreign Affairs, Subcommittee on International Organizations, Human Rights and Oversight. *U.N. Security Council Resolution 1325: Recognizing Women's Vital Roles in Achieving Peace and Security.* 110th Cong., 2nd sess., 15 May. Hearing transcript available at http://foreignaffairs.house.gov/hearing_notice.asp?id=988 (accessed 2 July 2010).

Women's Commission for Refugee Women and Children. 2006. *Beyond Firewood: Fuel Alternatives and Protection Strategies for Displaced Women and Girls.* March. New York: Women's Commission for Refugee Women and Children. Available at www.womensrefugeecommission.org/docs/fuel.pdf (accessed 2 July 2010).

United Nations

S/RES/1325 (2000)

Adopted by the Security Council at its 4213th meeting, on
31 October 2000

The Security Council,

Recalling its resolutions 1261 (1999) of 25 August 1999, 1265 (1999) of 17
September 1999, 1296 (2000) of 19 April 2000 and 1314 (2000) of 11
August 2000, as well as relevant statements of its President, and *recalling
also* the statement of its President to the press on the occasion of the
United Nations Day for Women's Rights and International Peace (Inter-
national Women's Day) of 8 March 2000 (SC/6816),

Recalling also the commitments of the Beijing Declaration and Platform
for Action (A/52/231) as well as those contained in the outcome document of the twenty-third Special Session of the United Nations General
Assembly entitled "Women 2000: Gender Equality, Development and
Peace for the Twenty-First Century" (A/S-23/10/Rev.1), in particular those
concerning women and armed conflict,

Bearing in mind the purposes and principles of the Charter of the United
Nations and the primary responsibility of the Security Council under the
Charter for the maintenance of international peace and security,

Expressing concern that civilians, particularly women and children, account for the vast majority of those adversely affected by armed conflict,
including as refugees and internally displaced persons, and increasingly
are targeted by combatants and armed elements, and *recognizing* the con-
sequent impact this has on durable peace and reconciliation,

Reaffirming the important role of women in the prevention and resolution of conflicts and in peace-building, and *stressing* the importance of
their equal participation and full involvement in all efforts for the maintenance and promotion of peace and security, and the need to increase
their role in decision-making with regard to conflict prevention and
resolution,

Reaffirming also the need to implement fully international humanitarian and human rights law that protects the rights of women and girls during and after conflicts,

Emphasizing the need for all parties to ensure that mine clearance and mine awareness programmes take into account the special needs of women and girls,

Recognizing the urgent need to mainstream a gender perspective into peacekeeping operations, and in this regard *noting* the Windhoek Declaration and the Namibia Plan of Action on Mainstreaming a Gender Perspective in Multidimensional Peace Support Operations (S/2000/693),

Recognizing also the importance of the recommendation contained in the statement of its President to the press of 8 March 2000 for specialized training for all peacekeeping personnel on the protection, special needs and human rights of women and children in conflict situations,

Recognizing that an understanding of the impact of armed conflict on women and girls, effective institutional arrangements to guarantee their protection and full participation in the peace process can significantly contribute to the maintenance and promotion of international peace and security,

Noting the need to consolidate data on the impact of armed conflict on women and girls,

1. *Urges* Member States to ensure increased representation of women at all decision-making levels in national, regional and international institutions and mechanisms for the prevention, management, and resolution of conflict;
2. *Encourages* the Secretary-General to implement his strategic plan of action (A/49/587) calling for an increase in the participation of women at decision-making levels in conflict resolution and peace processes;
3. *Urges* the Secretary-General to appoint more women as special representatives and envoys to pursue good offices on his behalf, and in this regard *calls on* Member States to provide candidates to the Secretary-General, for inclusion in a regularly updated centralized roster;
4. *Further urges* the Secretary-General to seek to expand the role and contribution of women in United Nations field-based operations, and especially among military observers, civilian police, human rights and humanitarian personnel;
5. *Expresses* its willingness to incorporate a gender perspective into peacekeeping operations, and *urges* the Secretary-General to ensure that, where appropriate, field operations include a gender component;

6. *Requests* the Secretary-General to provide to Member States training guidelines and materials on the protection, rights and the particular needs of women, as well as on the importance of involving women in all peacekeeping and peace-building measures, *invites* Member States to incorporate these elements as well as HIV/AIDS awareness training into their national training programmes for military and civilian police personnel in preparation for deployment, and *further requests* the Secretary-General to ensure that civilian personnel of peacekeeping operations receive similar training;

7. *Urges* Member States to increase their voluntary financial, technical and logistical support for gender-sensitive training efforts, including those undertaken by relevant funds and programmes, inter alia, the United Nations Fund for Women and United Nations Children's Fund, and by the Office of the United Nations High Commissioner for Refugees and other relevant bodies;

8. *Calls on* all actors involved, when negotiating and implementing peace agreements, to adopt a gender perspective, including, inter alia:
   (a) The special needs of women and girls during repatriation and re-settlement and for rehabilitation, reintegration and post-conflict reconstruction;
   (b) Measures that support local women's peace initiatives and indigenous processes for conflict resolution, and that involve women in all of the implementation mechanisms of the peace agreements;
   (c) Measures that ensure the protection of and respect for human rights of women and girls, particularly as they relate to the constitution, the electoral system, the police and the judiciary;

9. *Calls upon* all parties to armed conflict to respect fully international law applicable to the rights and protection of women and girls, especially as civilians, in particular the obligations applicable to them under the Geneva Conventions of 1949 and the Additional Protocols thereto of 1977, the Refugee Convention of 1951 and the Protocol thereto of 1967, the Convention on the Elimination of All Forms of Discrimination against Women of 1979 and the Optional Protocol thereto of 1999 and the United Nations Convention on the Rights of the Child of 1989 and the two Optional Protocols thereto of 25 May 2000, and to bear in mind the relevant provisions of the Rome Statute of the International Criminal Court;

10. *Calls on* all parties to armed conflict to take special measures to protect women and girls from gender-based violence, particularly rape and other forms of sexual abuse, and all other forms of violence in situations of armed conflict;

11. *Emphasizes* the responsibility of all States to put an end to impunity and to prosecute those responsible for genocide, crimes against humanity, and war crimes including those relating to sexual and other violence against women and girls, and in this regard *stresses* the need to exclude these crimes, where feasible from amnesty provisions;

12. *Calls upon* all parties to armed conflict to respect the civilian and humanitarian character of refugee camps and settlements, and to take into account the particular needs of women and girls, including in their design, and recalls its resolutions 1208 (1998) of 19 November 1998 and 1296 (2000) of 19 April 2000;

13. *Encourages* all those involved in the planning for disarmament, demobilization and reintegration to consider the different needs of female and male ex-combatants and to take into account the needs of their dependants;

14. *Reaffirms* its readiness, whenever measures are adopted under Article 41 of the Charter of the United Nations, to give consideration to their potential impact on the civilian population, bearing in mind the special needs of women and girls, in order to consider appropriate humanitarian exemptions;

15. *Expresses* its willingness to ensure that Security Council missions take into account gender considerations and the rights of women, including through consultation with local and international women's groups;

16. *Invites* the Secretary-General to carry out a study on the impact of armed conflict on women and girls, the role of women in peacebuilding and the gender dimensions of peace processes and conflict resolution, and *further invites* him to submit a report to the Security Council on the results of this study and to make this available to all Member States of the United Nations;

17. *Requests* the Secretary-General, where appropriate, to include in his reporting to the Security Council progress on gender mainstreaming throughout peacekeeping missions and all other aspects relating to women and girls;

18. *Decides* to remain actively seized of the matter.

United Nations

S/RES/1889 (2009)

Adopted by the Security Council at its 6196th meeting, on
5 October 2009

The Security Council,

Reaffirming its commitment to the continuing and full implementation, in a mutually reinforcing manner, of resolutions 1325 (2000), 1612 (2005), 1674 (2006), 1820 (2008), 1882 (2009), 1888 (2009) and all relevant Statements of its Presidents,

Guided by the purposes and principles of the Charter of the United Nations, and *bearing in mind* the primary responsibility of the Security Council under the Charter for the maintenance of international peace and security,

Recalling the resolve expressed in the 2005 United Nations General Assembly World Summit Outcome Document (A/RES/60/1) to eliminate all forms of violence against women and girls, the obligations of States Parties to the Convention on the Elimination of All Forms of Discrimination Against Women and the Optional Protocol thereto, the Convention on the Rights of the Child and the Optional Protocols thereto, *recalling also* the commitments contained in the Beijing Declaration and Platform for Action as well as those contained in the outcome document of the twenty-third Special Session of the United Nations General Assembly entitled "Women 2000: Gender Equality, Development and Peace for the Twenty-First Century" (A/S-23/10/Rev.1), in particular those concerning women and armed conflict,

Having considered the report of the Secretary General (S/2009/465) of 16 September 2009 and *stressing* that the present resolution does not seek to make any legal determination as to whether situations that are referred to in the Secretary General's report are or are not armed conflicts within the context of the Geneva Conventions and the Additional Protocols thereto, nor does it prejudice the legal status of the non-State parties involved in these situations,

Welcoming the efforts of Member States in implementing its resolution 1325 (2000) at the national level, including the development of national action plans, and *encouraging* Member States to continue to pursue such implementation,

Reiterating the need for the full, equal and effective participation of women at all stages of peace processes given their vital role in the prevention and resolution of conflict and peacebuilding, *reaffirming* the key role women can play in re-establishing the fabric of recovering society and *stressing* the need for their involvement in the development and implementation of post-conflict strategies in order to take into account their perspectives and needs,

Expressing deep concern about the under-representation of women at all stages of peace processes, particularly the very low numbers of women in formal roles in mediation processes and stressing the need to ensure that women are appropriately appointed at decision-making levels, as high level mediators, and within the composition of the mediators' teams,

Remaining deeply concerned about the persistent obstacles to women's full involvement in the prevention and resolution of conflicts and participation in post-conflict public life, as a result of violence and intimidation, lack of security and lack of rule of law, cultural discrimination and stigmatization, including the rise of extremist or fanatical views on women, and socio-economic factors including the lack of access to education, and in this respect, *recognizing* that the marginalization of women can delay or undermine the achievement of durable peace, security and reconciliation,

Recognizing the particular needs of women and girls in post-conflict situations, including, inter alia, physical security, health services including reproductive and mental health, ways to ensure their livelihoods, land and property rights, employment, as well as their participation in decision-making and post-conflict planning, particularly at early stages of post-conflict peacebuilding,

Noting that despite progress, obstacles to strengthening women's participation in conflict prevention, conflict resolution and peacebuilding remain, *expressing concern* that women's capacity to engage in public decision making and economic recovery often does not receive adequate recognition or financing in post-conflict situations, and *underlining* that funding for women's early recovery needs is vital to increase women's empowerment, which can contribute to effective post-conflict peacebuilding,

Noting that women in situations of armed conflict and post-conflict situations continue to be often considered as victims and not as actors in addressing and resolving situations of armed conflict and *stressing* the need to focus not only on protection of women but also on their empowerment in peacebuilding,

Recognizing that an understanding of the impact of situations of armed conflict on women and girls, including as refugees and internally displaced persons, adequate and rapid response to their particular needs, and effective institutional arrangements to guarantee their protection and full participation in the peace process, particularly at early stages of post-conflict peacebuilding, can significantly contribute to the maintenance and promotion of international peace and security,

Welcoming the United Nations initiative to develop a system similar to that pioneered by the United Nations Development Programme to allow decision-makers to track gender-related allocations in United Nations Development Group Multi-Donor Trust Funds,

Welcoming the efforts of the Secretary-General to appoint more women to senior United Nations positions, particularly in field missions, as a tangible step towards providing United Nations leadership on implementation of its resolution 1325 (2000),

Welcoming the upcoming establishment of a United Nations Steering Committee to enhance visibility and strengthen coordination within the United Nations system regarding the preparations for the 10th anniversary of resolution 1325 (2000),

Encouraging relevant actors to organize events during 2009–2010 at the global, regional and national levels to increase awareness about resolution 1325 (2000), including ministerial events, to renew commitments to "Women and peace and security," and to identify ways to address remaining and new challenges in implementing resolution 1325 (2000) in the future,

1. *Urges* Member States, international and regional organisations to take further measures to improve women's participation during all stages of peace processes, particularly in conflict resolution, post-conflict planning and peacebuilding, including by enhancing their engagement in political and economic decision-making at early stages of recovery processes, through inter alia promoting women's leadership and capacity to engage in aid management and planning, supporting women's organizations, and countering negative societal attitudes about women's capacity to participate equally;
2. *Reiterates* its call for all parties in armed conflicts to respect fully international law applicable to the rights and protection of women and girls;

3. *Strongly condemns* all violations of applicable international law committed against women and girls in situations of armed conflicts and post-conflict situations, *demands* all parties to conflicts to cease such acts with immediate effect, and *emphasizes* the responsibility of all States to put an end to impunity and to prosecute those responsible for all forms of violence committed against women and girls in armed conflicts, including rape and other sexual violence;

4. *Calls upon* the Secretary-General to develop a strategy, including through appropriate training, to increase the number of women appointed to pursue good offices on his behalf, particularly as Special Representatives and Special Envoys, and to take measures to increase women's participation in United Nations political, peacebuilding and peacekeeping missions;

5. *Requests* the Secretary-General to ensure that all country reports to the Security Council provide information on the impact of situations of armed conflict on women and girls, their particular needs in post-conflict situations and obstacles to attaining those needs;

6. *Requests* the Secretary-General to ensure that relevant United Nations bodies, in cooperation with Member States and civil society, collect data on, analyze and systematically assess particular needs of women and girls in post-conflict situations, including, inter alia, information on their needs for physical security and participation in decision-making and post-conflict planning, in order to improve system-wide response to those needs;

7. *Expresses* its intention, when establishing and renewing the mandates of United Nations missions, to include provisions on the promotion of gender equality and the empowerment of women in post-conflict situations, and *requests* the Secretary-General to continue, as appropriate, to appoint gender advisors and/or women-protection advisors to United Nations missions and asks them, in cooperation with United Nations Country Teams, to render technical assistance and improved coordination efforts to address recovery needs of women and girls in post-conflict situations;

8. *Urges* Member States to ensure gender mainstreaming in all post-conflict peacebuilding and recovery processes and sectors;

9. *Urges* Member States, United Nations bodies, donors and civil society to ensure that women's empowerment is taken into account during post-conflict needs assessments and planning, and factored into subsequent funding disbursements and programme activities, including through developing transparent analysis and tracking of funds allocated for addressing women's needs in the post-conflict phase;

10. *Encourages* Member States in post-conflict situations, in consultation with civil society, including women's organizations, to specify in detail women and girls' needs and priorities and design concrete strategies, in accordance with their legal systems, to address those needs and priorities, which cover inter alia support for greater physical security and better socio-economic conditions, through education, income generating activities, access to basic services, in particular health services, including sexual and reproductive health and reproductive rights and mental health, gender-responsive law enforcement and access to justice, as well as enhancing capacity to engage in public decision-making at all levels;

11. *Urges* Member States, United Nations bodies and civil society, including non-governmental organizations, to take all feasible measures to ensure women and girls' equal access to education in post-conflict situations, given the vital role of education in the promotion of women's participation in post-conflict decision-making;

12. *Calls upon* all parties to armed conflicts to respect the civilian and humanitarian character of refugee camps and settlements, and ensure the protection of all civilians inhabiting such camps, in particular women and girls, from all forms of violence, including rape and other sexual violence, and to ensure full, unimpeded and secure humanitarian access to them;

13. *Calls upon* all those involved in the planning for disarmament, demobilization and reintegration to take into account particular needs of women and girls associated with armed forces and armed groups and their children, and provide for their full access to these programmes;

14. *Encourages* the Peacebuilding Commission and Peacebuilding Support Office to continue to ensure systematic attention to and mobilisation of resources for advancing gender equality and women's empowerment as an integral part of post-conflict peacebuilding, and to encourage the full participation of women in this process;

15. *Requests* the Secretary-General, in his agenda for action to improve the United Nations' peacebuilding efforts, to take account of the need to improve the participation of women in political and economic decision-making from the earliest stages of the peacebuilding process;

16. *Requests* the Secretary-General to ensure full transparency, cooperation and coordination of efforts between the Special Representative of the Secretary-General on Children and Armed Conflict and the Special Representative of the Secretary General on sexual violence and armed conflict whose appointment has been requested by its resolution 1888 (2009);

17. *Requests* the Secretary-General to submit to the Security Council within 6 months, for consideration, a set of indicators for use at the

global level to track implementation of its resolution 1325 (2000), which could serve as a common basis for reporting by relevant United Nations entities, other international and regional organizations, and Member States, on the implementation of resolution 1325 (2000) in 2010 and beyond;

18. *Requests* the Secretary-General, within the report requested in S/PRST/2007/40, to also include a review of progress in the implementation of its resolution 1325 (2000), an assessment of the processes by which the Security Council receives, analyses and takes action on information pertinent to resolution 1325 (2000), recommendations on further measures to improve coordination across the United Nations system, and with Member States and civil society to deliver implementation, and data on women's participation in United Nations missions;

19. *Requests* the Secretary-General to submit a report to the Security Council within 12 months on addressing women's participation and inclusion in peacebuilding and planning in the aftermath of conflict, taking into consideration the views of the Peacebuilding Commission and to include, inter alia:

    a. Analysis on the particular needs of women and girls in post-conflict situations,

    b. Challenges to women's participation in conflict resolution and peacebuilding and gender mainstreaming in all early post-conflict planning, financing and recovery processes,

    c. Measures to support national capacity in planning for and financing responses to the needs of women and girls in post-conflict situations,

    d. Recommendations for improving international and national responses to the needs of women and girls in post-conflict situations, including the development of effective financial and institutional arrangements to guarantee women's full and equal participation in the peacebuilding process,

20. *Decides* to remain actively seized of the matter.

United Nations

S/RES/1820 (2008)

Adopted by the Security Council at its 5916th meeting, on
19 June 2008

The Security Council,

Reaffirming its commitment to the continuing and full implementation
of resolution 1325 (2000), 1612 (2005) and 1674 (2006) and recalling the
Statements of its president of 31 October 2001 (Security Council/
PRST/2001/31), 31 October 2002 (Security Council/PRST/2002/32), 28
October 2004 (Security Council/PRST/2004/40), 27 October 2005 (Se-
curity Council/PRST/2005/52), 8 November 2006 (Security Council/
PRST/2006/42), 7 March 2007 (Security Council/PRST/2007/5), and
24 October 2007 (Security Council/PRST/2007/40);

Guided by the purposes and principles of the Charter of the United
Nations,

Reaffirming also the resolve expressed in the 2005 World Summit Outcome Document to eliminate all forms of violence against women and
girls, including by ending impunity and by ensuring the protection of civilians, in particular women and girls, during and after armed conflicts,
in accordance with the obligations States have undertaken under international humanitarian law and international human rights law;

Recalling the commitments of the Beijing Declaration and Platform for
Action (A/52/231) as well as those contained in the outcome document of
the twenty-third Special Session of the United Nations General Assembly entitled "Women 2000: Gender Equality, Development and Peace for
the Twenty-first Century" (A/S-23/10/Rev.1), in particular those concerning sexual violence and women in situations of armed conflict;

Reaffirming also the obligations of States Parties to the Convention on
the Elimination of All Forms of Discrimination against Women, the Optional Protocol thereto, the Convention on the Rights of the Child and

the Optional Protocols thereto, and urging states that have not yet done so to consider ratifying or acceding to them,

Noting that civilians account for the vast majority of those adversely affected by armed conflict; that women and girls are particularly targeted by the use of sexual violence, including as a tactic of war to humiliate, dominate, instil fear in, disperse and/or forcibly relocate civilian members of a community or ethnic group; and that sexual violence perpetrated in this manner may in some instances persist after the cessation of hostilities;

Recalling its condemnation in the strongest terms of all sexual and other forms of violence committed against civilians in armed conflict, in particular women and children;

Reiterating deep concern that, despite its repeated condemnation of violence against women and children in situations of armed conflict, including sexual violence in situations of armed conflict, and despite its calls addressed to all parties to armed conflict for the cessation of such acts with immediate effect, such acts continue to occur, and in some situations have become systematic and widespread, reaching appalling levels of brutality,

Recalling the inclusion of a range of sexual violence offences in the Rome Statute of the International Criminal Court and the statutes of the ad hoc international criminal tribunals,

Reaffirming the important role of women in the prevention and resolution of conflicts and in peacebuilding, and *stressing* the importance of their equal participation and full involvement in all efforts for the maintenance and promotion of peace and security, and the need to increase their role in decision-making with regard to conflict prevention and resolution,

Deeply concerned also about the persistent obstacles and challenges to women's participation and full involvement in the prevention and resolution of conflicts as a result of violence, intimidation and discrimination, which erode women's capacity and legitimacy to participate in post-conflict public life, and acknowledging the negative impact this has on durable peace, security and reconciliation, including post-conflict peacebuilding,

Recognizing that States bear primary responsibility to respect and ensure the human rights of their citizens, as well as all individuals within their territory as provided for by relevant international law,

Reaffirming that parties to armed conflict bear the primary responsibility to take all feasible steps to ensure the protection of affected civilians,

Welcoming the ongoing coordination of efforts within the United Nations system, marked by the inter-agency initiative "United Nations Action against Sexual Violence in Conflict," to create awareness about sexual violence in armed conflicts and post-conflict situations and, ultimately, to put an end to it,

1. *Stresses* that sexual violence, when used or commissioned as a tactic of war in order to deliberately target civilians or as a part of a widespread or systematic attack against civilian populations, can significantly exacerbate situations of armed conflict and may impede the restoration of international peace and security, *affirms* in this regard that effective steps to prevent and respond to such acts of sexual violence can significantly contribute to the maintenance of international peace and security, and *expresses its readiness*, when considering situations on the agenda of the Council, to, where necessary, adopt appropriate steps to address widespread or systematic sexual violence;

2. *Demands* the immediate and complete cessation by all parties to armed conflict of all acts of sexual violence against civilians with immediate effect;

3. *Demands* that all parties to armed conflict immediately take appropriate measures to protect civilians, including women and girls, from all forms of sexual violence, which could include, inter alia, enforcing appropriate military disciplinary measures and upholding the principle of command responsibility, training troops on the categorical prohibition of all forms of sexual violence against civilians, debunking myths that fuel sexual violence, vetting armed and security forces to take into account past actions of rape and other forms of sexual violence, and evacuation of women and children under imminent threat of sexual violence to safety; and *requests* the Secretary-General, where appropriate, to encourage dialogue to address this issue in the context of broader discussions of conflict resolution between appropriate UN officials and the parties to the conflict, taking into account, inter alia, the views expressed by women of affected local communities;

4. *Notes* that rape and other forms of sexual violence can constitute a war crime, a crime against humanity, or a constitutive act with respect to genocide, *stresses the need for* the exclusion of sexual violence crimes from amnesty provisions in the context of conflict resolution processes, and *calls upon* Member States to comply with their obligations for prosecuting persons responsible for such acts, to ensure that all victims of sexual violence, particularly women and girls, have equal protection under the law and equal access to justice, and *stresses* the importance of

ending impunity for such acts as part of a comprehensive approach to seeking sustainable peace, justice, truth, and national reconciliation;

5. *Affirms its intention*, when establishing and renewing state-specific sanctions regimes, to take into consideration the appropriateness of targeted and graduated measures against parties to situations of armed conflict who commit rape and other forms of sexual violence against women and girls in situations of armed conflict;

6. *Requests* the Secretary-General, in consultation with the Security Council, the Special Committee on Peacekeeping Operations and its Working Group and relevant States, as appropriate, to develop and implement appropriate training programs for all peacekeeping and humanitarian personnel deployed by the United Nations in the context of missions as mandated by the Council to help them better prevent, recognize and respond to sexual violence and other forms of violence against civilians;

7. *Requests* the Secretary-General to continue and strengthen efforts to implement the policy of zero tolerance of sexual exploitation and abuse in United Nations peacekeeping operations; and *urges* troop and police contributing countries to take appropriate preventative action, including pre-deployment and in-theater awareness training, and other action to ensure full accountability in cases of such conduct involving their personnel;

8. *Encourages* troop and police contributing countries, in consultation with the Secretary-General, to consider steps they could take to heighten awareness and the responsiveness of their personnel participating in UN peacekeeping operations to protect civilians, including women and children, and prevent sexual violence against women and girls in conflict and post-conflict situations, including wherever possible the deployment of a higher percentage of women peacekeepers or police;

9. *Requests* the Secretary-General to develop effective guidelines and strategies to enhance the ability of relevant UN peacekeeping operations, consistent with their mandates, to protect civilians, including women and girls, from all forms of sexual violence and to systematically include in his written reports to the Council on conflict situations his observations concerning the protection of women and girls and recommendations in this regard;

10. *Requests* the Secretary-General and relevant United Nations agencies, inter alia, through consultation with women and women-led organizations as appropriate, to develop effective mechanisms for providing protection from violence, including in particular sexual violence, to women and girls in and around UN managed refugee

and internally displaced persons camps, as well as in all disarmament, demobilization, and reintegration processes, and in justice and security sector reform efforts assisted by the United Nations;

11. *Stresses* the important role the Peacebuilding Commission can play by including in its advice and recommendations for post-conflict peace-building strategies, where appropriate, ways to address sexual violence committed during and in the aftermath of armed conflict, and in en-suring consultation and effective representation of women's civil soci-ety in its country-specific configurations, as part of its wider approach to gender issues;

12. *Urges* the Secretary-General and his Special Envoys to invite women to participate in discussions pertinent to the prevention and resolution of conflict, the maintenance of peace and security, and post-conflict peacebuilding, and encourages all parties to such talks to facilitate the equal and full participation of women at decision-making levels;

13. *Urges* all parties concerned, including Member States, United Na-tions entities and financial institutions, to support the development and strengthening of the capacities of national institutions, in partic-ular of judicial and health systems, and of local civil society networks in order to provide sustainable assistance to victims of sexual violence in armed conflict and post-conflict situations;

14. *Urges* appropriate regional and sub-regional bodies in particular to consider developing and implementing policies, activities, and advo-cacy for the benefit of women and girls affected by sexual violence in armed conflict;

15. *Also requests* the Secretary-General to submit a report to the Coun-cil by 30 June 2009 on the implementation of this resolution in the context of situations which are on the agenda of the Council, utilizing information from available United Nations sources, including country teams, peacekeeping operations, and other United Nations personnel, which would include, inter alia, information on situations of armed conflict in which sexual violence has been widely or systematically em-ployed against civilians; analysis of the prevalence and trends of sexual violence in situations of armed conflict; proposals for strategies to mini-mize the susceptibility of women and girls to such violence; benchmarks for measuring progress in preventing and addressing sexual violence; appropriate input from United Nations implementing partners in the field; information on his plans for facilitating the collection of timely, objective, accurate, and reliable information on the use of sexual vio-lence in situations of armed conflict, including through improved co-ordination of UN activities on the ground and at Headquarters; and information on actions taken by parties to armed conflict to implement

their responsibilities as described in this resolution, in particular by immediately and completely ceasing all acts of sexual violence and in taking appropriate measures to protect women and girls from all forms of sexual violence;

16. *Decides* to remain actively seized of the matter.

United Nations

S/RES/1888 (2009)

Adopted by the Security Council at its 6195th meeting, on 30 September 2009

The Security Council,

Reaffirming its commitment to the continuing and full implementation of resolutions 1325 (2000), 1612 (2005), 1674 (2006), 1820 (2008) and 1882 (2009) and all relevant statements of its President,

Welcoming the report of the Secretary-General of 16 July 2009 (S/2009/362), but remaining deeply concerned over the lack of progress on the issue of sexual violence in situations of armed conflict in particular against women and children, notably against girls, and noting as documented in the Secretary-General's report that sexual violence occurs in armed conflicts throughout the world,

Reiterating deep concern that, despite its repeated condemnation of violence against women and children including all forms of sexual violence in situations of armed conflict, and despite its calls addressed to all parties to armed conflict for the cessation of such acts with immediate effect, such acts continue to occur, and in some situations have become systematic or widespread,

Recalling the commitments of the Beijing Declaration and Platform for Action (A/52/231) as well as those contained in the outcome document of the twenty-third Special Session of the United Nations General Assembly entitled "Women 2000: Gender Equality, Development and Peace for the Twenty-First Century" (A/S-23/10/Rev.1), in particular those concerning women and armed conflict,

Reaffirming the obligations of States Parties to the Convention on the Elimination of All Forms of Discrimination against Women, the Optional Protocol thereto, the Convention on the Rights of the Child and the Optional Protocols thereto, and urging states that have not yet done so to consider ratifying or acceding to them,

Recalling that international humanitarian law affords general protection to women and children as part of the civilian population during armed conflicts and special protection due to the fact that they can be placed particularly at risk,

Recalling the responsibilities of States to end impunity and to prosecute those responsible for genocide, crimes against humanity, war crimes and other egregious crimes perpetrated against civilians, and in this regard, noting with concern that only limited numbers of perpetrators of sexual violence have been brought to justice, while recognizing that in conflict and in post conflict situations national justice systems may be significantly weakened,

Reaffirming that ending impunity is essential if a society in conflict or recovering from conflict is to come to terms with past abuses committed against civilians affected by armed conflict and to prevent future such abuses, *drawing attention* to the full range of justice and reconciliation mechanisms to be considered, including national, international and "mixed" criminal courts and tribunals and truth and reconciliation commissions, and *noting* that such mechanisms can promote not only individual responsibility for serious crimes, but also peace, truth, reconciliation and the rights of the victims,

Recalling the inclusion of a range of sexual violence offences in the Rome Statute of the International Criminal Court and the statutes of the ad hoc international criminal tribunals,

Stressing the necessity for all States and non-State parties to conflicts to comply fully with their obligations under applicable international law, including the prohibition on all forms of sexual violence,

Recognizing the need for civilian and military leaders, consistent with the principle of command responsibility, to demonstrate commitment and political will to prevent sexual violence and to combat impunity and enforce accountability, and that inaction can send a message that the incidence of sexual violence in conflicts is tolerated,

Emphasizing the importance of addressing sexual violence issues from the outset of peace processes and mediation efforts, in order to protect populations at risk and promote full stability, in particular in the areas of pre-ceasefire humanitarian access and human rights agreements, ceasefires and ceasefire monitoring, Disarmament, Demobilization and Reintegration (DDR), Security Sector Reform (SSR) arrangements, justice and reparations, post-conflict recovery and development,

Noting with concern the underrepresentation of women in formal peace processes, the lack of mediators and ceasefire monitors with proper training in dealing with sexual violence, and the lack of women as Chief or Lead peace mediators in United Nations-sponsored peace talks,

Recognizing that the promotion and empowerment of women and that support for women's organizations and networks are essential in the consolidation of peace to promote the equal and full participation of women and *encouraging* Member States, donors, and civil society, including nongovernmental organizations, to provide support in this respect,

Welcoming the inclusion of women in peacekeeping missions in civil, military and police functions, and *recognizing* that women and children affected by armed conflict may feel more secure working with and reporting abuse to women in peacekeeping missions, and that the presence of women peacekeepers may encourage local women to participate in the national armed and security forces, thereby helping to build a security sector that is accessible and responsive to all, especially women,

Welcoming the efforts of the Department of Peacekeeping Operations to develop gender guidelines for military personnel in peacekeeping operations to facilitate the implementation of resolutions 1325 (2000) and 1820 (2008), and operational guidance to assist civilian, military and police components of peacekeeping missions to effectively implement resolution 1820 (2008),

Having considered the report of the Secretary-General of 16 July 2009 (S/2009/362) and *stressing* that the present resolution does not seek to make any legal determination as to whether situations that are referred to in the Secretary-General's report are or are not armed conflicts within the context of the Geneva Conventions and the Additional Protocols thereto, nor does it prejudge the legal status of the non-State parties involved in these situations,

Recalling the Council's decision in resolution 1882 of 4 August 2009 (S/RES/1882) to expand the Annexed list in the Secretary-General's annual report on Children and Armed Conflict of parties in situations of armed conflict engaged in the recruitment or use of children in violation of international law to also include those parties to armed conflict that engage, in contravention of applicable international law, in patterns of killing and maiming of children and/or rape and other sexual violence against children, in situations of armed conflict,

Noting the role currently assigned to the Office of the Special Adviser on Gender Issues to monitor implementation of resolution 1325 and to promote gender mainstreaming within the United Nations system, women's empowerment and gender equality, and *expressing* the importance of effective coordination within the United Nations system in these areas,

Recognizing that States bear the primary responsibility to respect and ensure the human rights of their citizens, as well as all individuals within their territory as provided for by relevant international law,

Reaffirming that parties to armed conflict bear the primary responsibility to take all feasible steps to ensure the protection of affected civilians,

Reiterating its primary responsibility for the maintenance of international peace and security and, in this connection, its commitment to continue to address the widespread impact of armed conflict on civilians, including with regard to sexual violence,

1. *Reaffirms* that sexual violence, when used or commissioned as a tactic of war in order to deliberately target civilians or as a part of a widespread or systematic attack against civilian populations, can significantly exacerbate situations of armed conflict and may impede the restoration of international peace and security; *affirms* in this regard that effective steps to prevent and respond to such acts of sexual violence can significantly contribute to the maintenance of international peace and security; and *expresses its readiness*, when considering situations on the agenda of the Council, to take, where necessary, appropriate steps to address widespread or systematic sexual violence in situations of armed conflict;

2. *Reiterates* its demand for the complete cessation by all parties to armed conflict of all acts of sexual violence with immediate effect;

3. *Demands* that all parties to armed conflict immediately take appropriate measures to protect civilians, including women and children, from all forms of sexual violence, including measures such as, inter alia, enforcing appropriate military disciplinary measures and upholding the principle of command responsibility, training troops on the categorical prohibition of all forms of sexual violence against civilians, debunking myths that fuel sexual violence and vetting candidates for national armies and security forces to ensure the exclusion of those associated with serious violations of international humanitarian and human rights law, including sexual violence;

4. *Requests* that the United Nations Secretary-General appoint a Special Representative to provide coherent and strategic leadership, to work effectively to strengthen existing United Nations coordination

mechanisms, and to engage in advocacy efforts, inter alia with governments, including military and judicial representatives, as well as with all parties to armed conflict and civil society, in order to address, at both headquarters and country level, sexual violence in armed conflict, while promoting cooperation and coordination of efforts among all relevant stakeholders, primarily through the inter-agency initiative "United Nations Action Against Sexual Violence in Conflict";

5. *Encourages* the entities comprising UN Action Against Sexual Violence in Conflict, as well as other relevant parts of the United Nations system, to support the work of the aforementioned Special Representative of the Secretary-General and to continue and enhance cooperation and information sharing among all relevant stakeholders in order to reinforce coordination and avoid overlap at the headquarters and country levels and improve system-wide response;

6. *Urges* States to undertake comprehensive legal and judicial reforms, as appropriate, in conformity with international law, without delay and with a view to bringing perpetrators of sexual violence in conflicts to justice and to ensuring that survivors have access to justice, are treated with dignity throughout the justice process and are protected and receive redress for their suffering;

7. *Urges* all parties to a conflict to ensure that all reports of sexual violence committed by civilians or by military personnel are thoroughly investigated and the alleged perpetrators brought to justice, and that civilian superiors and military commanders, in accordance with international humanitarian law, use their authority and powers to prevent sexual violence, including by combating impunity;

8. *Calls upon* the Secretary-General to identify and take the appropriate measures to deploy rapidly a team of experts to situations of particular concern with respect to sexual violence in armed conflict, working through the United Nations presence on the ground and with the consent of the host government, to assist national authorities to strengthen the rule of law, and *recommends* making use of existing human resources within the United Nations system and voluntary contributions, drawing upon requisite expertise, as appropriate, in the rule of law, civilian and military judicial systems, mediation, criminal investigation, security sector reform, witness protection, fair trial standards, and public outreach; to, inter alia:

   (a) Work closely with national legal and judicial officials and other personnel in the relevant governments' civilian and military justice systems to address impunity, including by the strengthening of national capacity, and drawing attention to the full range of justice mechanisms to be considered;

(b) Identify gaps in national response and encourage a holistic national approach to address sexual violence in armed conflict, including by enhancing criminal accountability, responsiveness to victims, and judicial capacity;

(c) Make recommendations to coordinate domestic and international efforts and resources to reinforce the government's ability to address sexual violence in armed conflict;

(d) Work with the United Nations Mission, Country Team, and the aforementioned Special Representative of the Secretary-General as appropriate towards the full implementation of the measures called for by resolution 1820 (2008);

9. *Encourages* States, relevant United Nations entities and civil society, as appropriate, to provide assistance in close cooperation with national authorities to build national capacity in the judicial and law enforcement systems in situations of particular concern with respect to sexual violence in armed conflict;

10. *Reiterates its intention*, when adopting or renewing targeted sanctions in situations of armed conflict, to consider including, where appropriate, designation criteria pertaining to acts of rape and other forms of sexual violence; and *calls* upon all peacekeeping and other relevant United Nations missions and United Nations bodies, in particular the Working Group on Children and Armed Conflict, to share with relevant United Nations Security Council sanctions committees, including through relevant United Nations Security Council Sanction Committees' monitoring groups and groups of experts, all pertinent information about sexual violence;

11. *Expresses its intention* to ensure that resolutions to establish or renew peacekeeping mandates contain provisions, as appropriate, on the prevention of, and response to, sexual violence, with corresponding reporting requirements to the Council;

12. *Decides* to include specific provisions, as appropriate, for the protection of women and children from rape and other sexual violence in the mandates of United Nations peacekeeping operations, including, on a case-by-case basis, the identification of women's protection advisers (WPAs) among gender advisers and human rights protection units, and requests the Secretary-General to ensure that the need for, and the number and roles of WPAs are systematically assessed during the preparation of each United Nations peacekeeping operation;

13. *Encourages* States, with the support of the international community, to increase access to health care, psychosocial support, legal assistance and socio economic reintegration services for victims of sexual violence, in particular in rural areas;

14. *Expresses* its intention to make better usage of periodical field visits to conflict areas, through the organization of interactive meetings with the local women and women's organizations in the field about the concerns and needs of women in areas of armed conflict;

15. *Encourages* leaders at the national and local level, including traditional leaders where they exist and religious leaders, to play a more active role in sensitizing communities on sexual violence to avoid marginalization and stigmatization of victims, to assist with their social reintegration, and to combat a culture of impunity for these crimes;

16. *Urges* the Secretary General, Member States and the heads of regional organizations to take measures to increase the representation of women in mediation processes and decision-making processes with regard to conflict resolution and peacebuilding;

17. *Urges* that issues of sexual violence be included in all United Nations-sponsored peace negotiation agendas, and *also urges* inclusion of sexual violence issues from the outset of peace processes in such situations, in particular in the areas of pre-ceasefires, humanitarian access and human rights agreements, ceasefires and ceasefire monitoring, DDR and SSR arrangements, vetting of armed and security forces, justice, reparations, and recovery/development;

18. *Reaffirms* the role of the Peacebuilding Commission in promoting inclusive gender-based approaches to reducing instability in post-conflict situations, noting the important role of women in rebuilding society, and *urges* the Peacebuilding Commission to encourage all parties in the countries on its agenda to incorporate and implement measures to reduce sexual violence in post-conflict strategies;

19. *Encourages* Member States to deploy greater numbers of female military and police personnel to United Nations peacekeeping operations, and to provide all military and police personnel with adequate training to carry out their responsibilities;

20. *Requests* the Secretary-General to ensure that technical support is provided to troop and police contributing countries, in order to include guidance for military and police personnel on addressing sexual violence in predeployment and induction training;

21. *Requests* the Secretary-General to continue and strengthen efforts to implement the policy of zero tolerance of sexual exploitation and abuse in United Nations peacekeeping operations; and *urges* troop and police contributing countries to take appropriate preventative action, including predeployment and in-theater awareness training, and other action to ensure full accountability in cases of such conduct involving their personnel;

22. *Requests* that the Secretary-General continue to direct all relevant United Nations entities to take specific measures to ensure systematic mainstreaming of gender issues within their respective institutions, including by ensuring allocation of adequate financial and human resources within all relevant offices and departments and on the ground, as well as to strengthen, within their respective mandates, their cooperation and coordination when addressing the issue of sexual violence in armed conflict;

23. *Urges* relevant Special Representatives and the Emergency Relief Coordinator of the Secretary-General, with strategic and technical support from the UN Action network, to work with Member States to develop joint Government-United Nations Comprehensive Strategies to Combat Sexual Violence, in consultation with all relevant stakeholders, and to regularly provide updates on this in their standard reporting to Headquarters;

24. *Requests* that the Secretary-General ensure more systematic reporting on incidents of trends, emerging patterns of attack, and early warning indicators of the use of sexual violence in armed conflict in all relevant reports to the Council, and *encourages* the Special Representatives of the Secretary-General, the Emergency Relief Coordinator, the High Commissioner for Human Rights, the Special Rapporteur on Violence against Women, and the Chairperson(s) of UN Action to provide, in coordination with the aforementioned Special Representative, additional briefings and documentation on sexual violence in armed conflict to the Council;

25. *Requests* the Secretary-General to include, where appropriate, in his regular reports on individual peacekeeping operations, information on steps taken to implement measures to protect civilians, particularly women and children, against sexual violence;

26. *Requests* the Secretary-General, taking into account the proposals contained in his report as well as any other relevant elements, to devise urgently and preferably within three months, specific proposals on ways to ensure monitoring and reporting in a more effective and efficient way within the existing United Nations system on the protection of women and children from rape and other sexual violence in armed conflict and post-conflict situations, utilizing expertise from the United Nations system and the contributions of national Governments, regional organizations, non-governmental organizations in their advisory capacity and various civil society actors, in order to provide timely, objective, accurate and reliable information on gaps in United Nations entities response, for consideration in taking appropriate action;

27. *Requests* that the Secretary-General continue to submit annual reports to the Council on the implementation of Resolution 1820 (2008) and to submit his next report by September of 2010 on the implementation of this resolution and Resolution 1820 (2008) to include, inter alia:
    (a) a detailed coordination and strategy plan on the timely and ethical collection of information;
    (b) updates on efforts by United Nations Mission focal points on sexual violence to work closely with the Resident Coordination/ Humanitarian Coordinator (RC/HC), the United Nations Country Team, and, where appropriate, the aforementioned Special Representative and/or the Team of Experts, to address sexual violence;
    (c) information regarding parties to armed conflict that are credibly suspected of committing patterns of rape or other forms of sexual violence, in situations that are on the Council's agenda;
28. *Decides* to review, taking into account the process established by General Assembly resolution 63/311 regarding a United Nations composite gender entity, the mandates of the Special Representative requested in operative paragraph 4 and the Team of Experts in operative paragraph 8 within two years, and as appropriate thereafter;
29. *Decides* to remain actively seized of the matter.

Contributors

Sanam Anderlini is the cofounder of the International Civil Society Action Network (ICAN), a U.S.-based NGO dedicated to supporting civil society activism in peace and security in conflict-affected countries. For more than a decade she has been a leading international advocate, researcher, trainer, and writer on conflict prevention and peacebuilding. In 2000 she was among civil society drafters of UN Security Council Resolution 1325 on women, peace, and security. Between 2002 and 2005, as Director of the Women Waging Peace Policy Commission, Anderlini led groundbreaking field research on women's contributions to conflict prevention, security, and peacemaking in twelve countries. Since 2005 she has also provided strategic guidance and training to key UN agencies, the U.K. government, and NGOs worldwide. In 2008 she was appointed as lead consultant for a new United Nations Development Programme global initiative, "Men and the Gendered Dimensions of Violence in Crisis Contexts." In 2009 she was appointed as a personal representative of the UN secretary-general to the Advisory Board of the UN Democracy Fund (UNDEF). In 2010 she was appointed to the Civil Society Advisory Group on Resolution 1325, chaired by Mary Robinson. Anderlini is also currently a research associate at the MIT Center for International Studies. She has written extensively on conflict issues, including as coauthor of *Civil War, Civil Peace* (Pluto Press, 1998); her most recent book is *Women Building Peace: What They Do, Why It Matters* (Lynne Rienner Publishers, 2007). Anderlini holds an MPhil in social anthropology from Cambridge University.

Tilman Brück is head of the Department of International Economics at the German Institute for Economic Research (DIW Berlin) and professor of development economics at Humboldt University Berlin. His research interests include the economics of household behavior and well-being in conflict and post-conflict economies and the economics of terrorism and insecurity. Brück is a cofounder and codirector of the Households in Conflict Network (HiCN; www.hicn.org) and the coordinator of the Economics of Security Initiative (www.economics-of-security.eu). He has also worked as a consultant for the European Commission, U.K. Department for International Development, Deutsche Gesellschaft für Technische Zusammenarbeit, International Labor Organization, German Development Bank, Organization for Economic Cooperation and Development, United Nations Development Programme, and U.S. Agency for International Development. Professor Brück is a research associate of the Poverty Research Unit at Sussex (PRUS) and of the Brooks World Poverty Institute (BWPI) at the University of Manchester, a research fellow at the Institute for the Study of Labor (IZA), an elected fellow of the German Young Academy of Sciences, and its chair in 2009–10. Brück studied economics at Glasgow University and Oxford University and obtained his doctorate in economics from Oxford University.

Helga Hernes is a senior adviser on women, peace, and security issues at the Peace Research Institute Oslo (PRIO). She also serves as a part-time chair of the Norwegian Parliamentary Intelligence Oversight Committee. She has previously been director of a number of programs at various research institutes in Norway, including executive director of the Center for International Climate and Energy Research, Oslo (CICERO), and research director of the Institute for Social Research, Oslo. She has published articles and books on a variety of topics, including international relations, multinational corporations, and the welfare state. Her work has been published in a number of languages and she has lectured in many countries. Hernes has also had a political and diplomatic career. For two periods (1988–89 and 1990–93) she served as state secretary at the Norwegian Ministry of Foreign Affairs, and from 1996 to 1998 she served as special adviser for UN peacekeeping operations. From 1998 to 2003 she was appointed as Norwegian ambassador to Austria and Slovakia, and from 2002 to 2004 as Norwegian ambassador to Switzerland and the Vatican. Hernes has also served on a number of public boards and commissions in Norway and other Scandinavian countries, as well as in the United States and Europe, both in the field of social science and policy research and in a public service capacity. She holds a master's degree and PhD in political science from Johns Hopkins University.

Chantal de Jonge Oudraat is director of the Jennings Randolph Fellowship Program. Before joining the U.S. Institute of Peace, de Jonge Oudraat was an adjunct associate professor at the Edmund A. Walsh School of Foreign Service, Georgetown University, and a senior fellow at the Center for Transatlantic Relations, Paul H. Nitze School of Advanced International Studies, Johns Hopkins University, where she focused on transatlantic relations and global security issues. In 2002, she was a recipient of the Robert Bosch Foundation Research Scholar Fellowship at the American

Institute for Contemporary German Studies (AICGS), Johns Hopkins University. She has also served as codirector of the Managing Global Issues project at the Carnegie Endowment for International Peace in Washington, DC (1998–2002); as research affiliate at the Belfer Center for Science and International Affairs, John F. Kennedy School of Government, Harvard University (1994–98); and a member of the directing staff at the United Nations Institute for Disarmament Research (UNIDIR) in Geneva (1981–94). De Jonge Oudraat is a member of Women in International Security (WIIS) and served on its executive board (1998–2007) and as its vice president (2001–07). She received her BA in political and social sciences from the University of Amsterdam, her MA from the University of Paris I (Sorbonne), and her PhD in political science from the University of Paris II (Panthéon).

Kathleen Kuehnast directs the Gender and Peacebuilding Center of Innovation. Kuehnast joined the U.S. Institute of Peace in January 2008 as associate vice president of the Grants Program following a fifteen-year career in international development. She has worked extensively with the World Bank, including managing international research projects and advising policymakers (government and nongovernment) on social development concerns, with a focus on gender-related issues. Her ongoing research focuses on the increasing socioeconomic disparities between men and women in Central Asia and their impact on local-level conflicts. As a recipient of the Mellon Foreign Fellowship at the Library of Congress in 2000 and the Kennan Institute for Advanced Russian Studies Fellowship at the Woodrow Wilson International Center for Scholars in 1999, she has studied and written extensively on the impact of post-Soviet transition on Muslim women of Central Asia. Her publications include *Post-Soviet Women Encountering Change: Nation Building, Economic Survival, and Civic Activism,* coedited with Carol Nechemias (Woodrow Wilson Center Press/Johns Hopkins University Press, 2004); *Better a Hundred Friends Than a Hundred Rubles? Social Networks in Transition—The Kyrgyz Republic,* coauthored with Nora Dudwick (World Bank, 2004); and *Whose Rules Rule? Everyday Border Conflicts in Central Asia,* coauthored with Nora Dudwick (Kennan Institute, 2008). Kuehnast holds a PhD in sociocultural anthropology from the University of Minnesota.

Inger Skjelsbæk is senior researcher and deputy director at the Peace Research Institute Oslo (PRIO). Her research interests include gender studies, political psychology, peace and conflict research, and research methodology. Skjelsbæk has published several articles in international academic journals, including *European Journal of International Relations, International Feminist Journal of Politics, Peace and Conflict: Journal of Peace Psychology,* and *International Peacekeeping.* She has also edited two books and has written numerous book chapters. In addition, she has published a number of reports and press commentaries, and frequently appears as a commentator and a lecturer, both domestically and internationally. Skjelsbæk maintains strong links with the University of Oslo, where she supervises masters and doctoral students and gives regular guest lectures, and has also been a visiting researcher at the University of California, Berkeley. Skjelsbæk has received research grants from, among other entities, the Fulbright Foundation, the Norwegian Ministry of Foreign Affairs, and the Research Council of Norway. Skjelsbæk is currently working on a multiyear project focusing on perpetrators of crimes of sexual violence during the Bosnian war. In 2012 she will be a guest researcher at the Human Rights Center at University of California, Berkeley, where she will write up her research findings from this project in a monograph for international publication. In addition, she is developing a new multiyear project, involving international collaboration, that focuses on the documentation of sexual violence in war. Skjelsbæk holds a doctorate in psychology from the Norwegian University of Science and Technology (NTNU).

Donald Steinberg was appointed deputy administrator of USAID in October 2010. Prior to this, he was deputy president for policy at the International Crisis Group, responsible for advocacy, policy formulation, and reporting for this nongovernmental organization charged with preventing and ending armed conflict. He previously directed the group's New York office. In 2005, he was a senior fellow at the U.S. Institute of Peace addressing issues of internal displacement, focusing on Sri Lanka, Kosovo, Sudan, and Colombia. During three decades with the U.S. diplomatic service, he served as ambassador to Angola, director of the State Department's Joint Policy Council, special representative of the president for humanitarian demining, special Haiti coordinator, deputy White House press secretary, and special assistant for African affairs to President Bill Clinton. Other diplomatic postings included South Africa, Mauritius, Malaysia, Brazil, and the Central African Republic. His awards include the Presidential Meritorious Honor Award, the Frasure Award for International Peace, a Pulitzer Traveling Fellowship, and six State Department Superior Honor Awards. He is a member of the UN Civil Society Advisory Group on Women, Peace and Security, and a board member of the Women's Refugee Commission. He holds master's degrees in journalism from Columbia University and political economy from University of Toronto, and a bachelor's degree from Reed College.

Marc Vothknecht is a research associate of the Department of International Economics at the German Institute for Economic Research (DIW Berlin). He is currently pursuing his doctorate in development economics at Humboldt University Berlin. His research addresses the social and economic legacies of violent conflicts, focusing in particular on the micro foundations of mass violence. Drawing on quantitative methods, his dissertation examines the episodes of conflict that have plagued Indonesia in the early post-Suharto era. He studied economics at the University of Göttingen, Germany, and at the University of Rennes 1, France.

Elisabeth Jean Wood is professor of political science at Yale University and professor at the Santa Fe Institute, where she teaches courses on comparative politics, political violence, social movements, and qualitative research methods. She is currently writing a book on sexual violence during war, drawing on field research in several countries. She is the author of *Forging Democracy from Below: Insurgent Transitions in South Africa and El Salvador* (Cambridge University Press, 2000) and *Insurgent Collective Action and Civil War in El Salvador* (Cambridge University Press, 2003). Among her recent articles are "Sexual Violence during War: Toward an Understanding of Variation," in *Order, Conflict, and Violence,* edited by Ian Shapiro, Stathis Kalyvas, and Tarek Masoud (Cambridge University Press, 2008); "Armed Groups and Sexual Violence: When Is Wartime Rape Rare?" (*Politics and Society,* 2009); "The Social Processes of Civil War: The Wartime Transformation of Social Networks" (*Annual Review of Political Science,* 2008); and "Revisiting Counterinsurgency," coauthored with Daniel Branch (*Politics and Society,* 2010). She serves on the editorial boards of *Politics and Society, The American Political Science Review,* and the Contentious Politics series of Cambridge University Press.

Index

About the Gender and Peacebuilding Center

Recognizing the importance and need for progress in women's contributions to peacebuilding, the United States Institute of Peace (USIP) established the Gender and Peacebuilding Center. The Center coordinates USIP's gender-related work. It aims to inform and expand critical understanding about the impact of gender; convene global experts on gender, conflict, and peacebuilding; contribute to policy development through analytical and practitioner work on gender, conflict, and peacebuilding; and enhance the role of women in peacebuilding by educating and training both men and women. Over the past twenty-five years, USIP has engaged in or supported more than one hundred projects related to women, conflict, and peacebuilding. The establishment of the Gender and Peacebuilding Center reflects the Institute's commitment to gender awareness in both its analytical and practitioner work on conflict and peacebuilding.

About the Peace Research Institute Oslo

Founded in 1959, the Peace Research Institute Oslo (PRIO) is an independent research institute known for its effective synergy of basic and policy-relevant research. In addition to undertaking such research, PRIO conducts graduate training and is engaged in the promotion of peace through conflict resolution, dialogue and reconciliation, public information, and policy-making activities.

About the United States Institute of Peace

The United States Institute of Peace is an independent, nonpartisan, national institution established and funded by Congress. Its goals are to help prevent and resolve violent international conflicts; promote post-conflict stability and development; and increase conflict management capacity, tools, and intellectual capital worldwide. The Institute pursues this mission by empowering others with knowledge, skills, and resources, as well as by directly engaging in peacebuilding efforts around the globe.

Board of Directors